Makers of Kenya's History

Olonana Ole Mbatian

Makers of Kenya's History

SERIES EDITOR: PROF. SIMIYU WANDIBBA

Makers of Kenya's History

Olonana Ole Mbatian

Peter Ndege

E.A.E.P

EAST AFRICAN EDUCATIONAL PUBLISHERS
Nairobi • Kampala • Dar es Salaam

Published by
East African Educational Publishers Ltd.
Brick Court, Mpaka Road/Woodvale Grove,
Westlands, P.O. Box 45314, Nairobi

East African Educational Publishers Ltd.
P.O. Box 11542, Kampala

Ujuzi Educational Publishers Ltd.
P.O. Box 31647, Kijito Nyama,
Dar es Salaam

First published 2003

ISBN 9966 25 094 8

Cover Illustration by John Nyagah

Printed in Kenya by Fotoform Ltd.
Muthithi House, Muthithi Road, P.O. Box 14681, Nairobi

Contents

Preface

Although the Maasai are the most studied community in Kenya, historians have hardly written about any of their leaders in a comprehensive manner. Only two brief biographies have been written on Maasai leaders. One, written by T. A. Kanyangezi, is on Mbatian, Olonana's father.[1] The other, written by Kenneth King, is on Molonket Olokorinya ole Sampele, a pioneer Christian[2]. The neglect is inexcusable since Maasai leaders, like those from other communities, have made important contributions to the making of the country's history. They have done this by being active actors in certain important events that shaped the future of Kenya in pre-colonial, colonial and post-colonial times. More specifically they imagined what the Maasai community ought to be like and defined the charters of the community and its relations with its neighbours and outsiders. In short, certain Maasai leaders contributed to Kenya's history by playing the role of statesmen and diplomats and, therefore, shaped important events that molded not only their community but also the whole country. In the course of this, they were themselves shaped by the events. They became prominent individuals because, through their actions, they were part of the conjecture, the building blocks which made Kenyan history.

Olonana ole Mbatian, the focus of this book, is a good example of a prominent Maasai and Kenyan leader. He lived during a very crucial period in Kenya's history. This was between the second half of the nineteenth century and the first decade of the twentieth century. During this period, the Maasai like other Kenyan communities were engaged in nation-building. They found themselves embroiled in internal competition for leadership and land, people and livestock, wealth and power. They also intermarried and exchanged commodities, ideas and culture. There were a series of disastrous famines, droughts and diseases to which they responded in different ways with many consequences.

Then came the foreign intruders, the Europeans armed with new commodities, weapons, ideas and cultural practices, and a more grandiose notion of nation-building: imperialism and capitalism take back. These intruders set to conquer Kenyan communities, using all the machinery. The Maasai, like other Kenyan communities, also responded indifferently. Their leaders played very important roles in the events that followed.

This book attempts to answer three fundamental questions regarding Olonana. First, to what extent, was he a product of his time? Second, how and to what extent did he shape events in Maasailand? Finally, what were his achievements and lasting legacy in Maasailand and the rest of Kenya?

In writing this book, I have mostly relied on the wide range of published works on the Maasai that cover themes such as the social, economic and political organization of the Maasai, the nineteenth century Maasai wars, drought and disease in Maasailand, alliance with the British and the oral literature of the Maasai. I would especially like to acknowledge the works of individuals like Alan Jacob, Richard Waller, John Galaty, Paul Spencer and Peter Rigby. Ole Sankan, Naomi Kipury, A. Ol' Oloisolo Masek and J. O. Sidai, to mention but a few scholars who have made valuable contribution to Maasai studies in general and, in particular, to my understanding of the subject of this study. It is from these works that I gleaned the basic facts abouth the Maasai and Olonana. Kipury's book introduced me to the primordial wisdom of the Maasai as rendered through their proverbs. This is not to trivialize the contribution of other scholars, listed in the end of each chapter and in the bibliography of this book. Their works also helped clarify a number of complex issues regarding the Maasai.

Apart from published materials, I also consulted a few British Foreign Office records availed by Professor Robert Maxon. The district annual reports for Laikipia and the Southern Maasai Reserve at the Kenya National Archives provided very valuable information. Some of these sources, particularly those that contain specific information on Olonana, have never been thoroughly analyzed. Their use, therefore, enabled me to make some original contribution to the biography of Olonana.

This study also benefited from the assistance of three of my former undergraduate students at Moi University, namely, Isaac ole Seret, David Sanaika ole Kinayia and Richard ole Tenkile. When they learnt that I was writing on Olonana they volunteered to collect oral information on the subject.

While writing about Olonana, I realized that I was also writing a history on the Maasai covering about forty years. A biography such as this, therefore, sheds some light on the community's as well as the national history. However, this is a long period in any community's history and I cannot therefore, claim to have done full justice to the subject. It is for this reason that I would like to state that what I have written about Olonana in this book is not exhaustive. It is merely an introductory work which must be improved by a more detailed study in future.

Peter Ndege
MOI UNIVERSITY
OCTOBER, 2002

Lenana; paramount chief of the Masai

Chapter One

Maasailand of Olonana's Youth: 1870 - 89

Like everybody else born in Maasailand during the second half of the nineteenth century, Olonana was very much influenced by the social, economic and political organization of the Maasai and the civil wars between the different sections of the community. Unlike other people, however, Olonana was also influenced by the special position his family occupied in the community, and, indeed, his own responses to the world around him. This chapter analyses the interplay of these factors and their influence on Olonana during the first nineteen or so years of his life.

Birth and childhood

Olonana was born around 1870 into a large extended family that belonged to a prophetic lineage, the Inkidongi of the Ilaiser clan. His father Mbatian, was a great prophet. Being his mother's only son, Mbatian must have desired to compensate for this by raising a large family. He married many wives, said to have been about one hundred, from different parts of Maasailand. Olonana's mother was either from Ilkaputei or Ilkisongo. His half-brothers included Senteu (Mbatian's most favourite son whose mother was also the favourite wife), Ngaroya, Endikita, Lasaloan and Ngabwel. Olonana's cousin, Ngaroya, and his uncle, Naliyang, would in later years be quite close to him and play an important role in his rise to power.

Like all male children, Olonana was quite a welcome addition to Mbatian's large family since the Maasai really valued children. Children bestowed status and respect on their parents and were used to establish stock friendship in the hope that the male and the female children in question would marry in future. The value of children is testified to by Maasai proverbs about them. For instance, the saying "children are the bright moon" (*Olapa oibor inkera*) means that children bring pleasure to the home.[1] Another proverb, "he who has

1

children cannot sleep in the bush" (*Meirrag tentim otoishe*) which means that children are important for they will take good care of their parents.[2]

Other proverbs specifically emphasize the value of male children. For instance, "Your son is the one for whom you found a wife" (*Pooki olaiyani lino oliyomaka*) meaning people marry not just to have children but, in particular, males.[3] The greater value attributed to male sons like Olonana, can be explained in terms of the highly patriarchal nature of the Maasai community. To counteract this tendency, the Maasai were urged, as the following proverb states, to love their children equally: "There is neither a child of the belly nor a child of the back" (*Meetae enkerai enkoshoke o enenkoriong*).[4] Most Maasai, as people in many other pre-industrial communities, found it almost impossible to heed this cautionary adage. Mbatian's disproportionate love for Senteu was, therefore, not an exceptional paternal sentiment.Many other patriarchs like him, either privately or openly, showed love to one son. Within the extended family, however, the unfavoured son had a wide range of relatives from whom he chose friends.

Olonana grew up among many uncles, mothers and cousins. This greatly influenced his upbringing. Right from childhood, he learned to live with people. He learned that even among close relatives, one still made friends as he did with Naliyang and Ngaroya. The others may not have been particularly friendly, but he had to learn to live with them. One had to be good-natured and tolerant without necessarily sacrificing self-interest. It was from this experience that Olonana drew strategies that he would use in his struggle with Senteu for leadership in later years.

Like other communities in pre-colonial Kenya, a child's upbringing among the Maasai was a collective responsibility although ultimate responsibility lay with the mother. During his childhood, Olonana spent more time in his mother's house, performing the chores that were required of him. His mother taught him the virtues of being respectful to his seniors. She punished him for errant behaviour but also protected him from ill-luck that might be caused by his jealous stepmothers and uncles. Sometimes, even his own father, in a fit of rage, would hurl a curse at him. His mother would neutralize the spell. Most of the time, however, Mbatian used his charm and ritual powers to protect the entire family, including the household of Olonana's mother.

As a child, Olonana never saw much of his father, though. It took quite a while before Mbatian actually came to his mother's house to perform the conjugal role given that he had to make rounds in all the households. And when Olonana's mother had her turn, the young Olonana was expected by custom to be out of the house as soon as his father stepped inside. Olonana remained one of his many children until he was about fifteen years old and ready for circumcision.

The young Olonana witnessed innumerable visits by people who came to consult Mbatian over a number of issues. Some of these people, particularly those from his mother's place, would put up in his mother's house as they waited for their turn to consult his father over a raid, war, or ritual arrangements. Initially, he may not have been able to understand what was going on around him but with time he did. With time he would be apprenticed into the intricacies of his father's prophetic and magical practice. He would also learn about his prophetic ancestry.

After he had learned and mastered the oral traditions of his people, Olonana could trace his own ancestry, as all male children in Mbatian's homesteads were expected to do. His lineage dated back to many generations from his father Mbatian to Kidongoi, the first great prophet, *Oloiboni kitok*. In between, he could count his other ancestors such as Supet, his own immediate grandfather, Sitonik, Kerika, Kipepeti, Parinyombi, Mweiya, and Lesigereishi, in that order. Olonana learnt also that his eponymous ancestor, Kidongoi, was not a Maasai but a foreigner who was found while on a lonely sojourn on a hill, most likely, Ngong, by a Maasai warrior in 1640. He learnt that Kidongoi was soon adopted by the Ilaiser clan because of his prophetic and magical.powers.[5] It was the infusion of the *oloiboni* institution into

3

the Maasai social formation, its historical development and the role within the community, that would be of greatest significance to Olonana when he later succeeded his father.

Traditional Maasai economy and society

Olonana was brought up in a community that was characterized by a complex system of social and political relationship which was based on the kinship system, the institution of the prophet (*Oloiboni*) and the age-grade and age-set systems. During the nineteenth century, the different sections of the Maasai community were involved in civil wars. In spite of this, more positive aspects of the community, its openness and inclusiveness as well as its egalitarian tendencies remained resilient. The dominant material base that influenced the manner in which these forces interacted to determine the course of the history of the Maasai, as well as Olonana's youthful experiences, was pastoralism. In later years, the necessity of protecting Maasai pastoralists against the ravages of epidemics and the covetousness of European settlers regarding the people's land would be a major challenge to Olonana's position as a *laibon*.

Pastoralism

Pastoralism influenced Olonana's upbringing and constituted a challenge to his leadership in later years. This was primarily due to its historical importance among the Maasai. According to Richard Waller, pastoralism was "the bedrock on which Maasai society rested... It not only shaped the way in which the Maasai society organized, permeated its institutions, and influenced the course of its development, but also provided the basis of a common identity and ideological underpinning for the Maasai community."[6] Livestock played economic, socio-political and religious roles as attested to by Maasai proverbs about cattle. The Maasai saying, "One cow is equal to a man's head" (*Erosore enkiteng nabo elukunya olee!*) was meant to signify some "equivalence" between a person and a cow.[7] This proverb emphasized the fact that livestock were a medium by which marital contracts were

4

made. They played a vital role in the growth of the community. Cows reproduced and were exchanged for women who, in turn, produced children who became members of the community.

Livestock was also exchanged for items such as spears, arrows, ornaments, and agricultural commodities. They were a store of value and, therefore, a means to accumulate wealth. So, the Maasai also said: "He that steps on cow-dung does not die" (*Meye olororita modiok*).[8] Plenty of cow-dung, particularly in one's homestead, symbolized the possession of livestock and, by implication, wealth and health. Due to the intrinsic value of livestock the Maasai were prepared to fight to acquire and defend cattle. This found expression in the proverb, "It is the bow that tends cattle" (*Enkawuo nabar kishu*).[9] But it also found concrete demonstration during Olonana's own lifetime in the Maasai civil wars. Pastoralism had penetrated all the pores of Maasai social formation and become extremely important. This was largely because of its antiquity and the manner in which it influenced the organization of the community.

By the nineteenth century, pastoralism had existed in East Africa for over four thousand years. The Maasai had been associated with it since their arrival and settlement in mush of the Rift Valley, between 1200 and 1500 A.D. Their commitment to pastoralism by the middle of the seventeenth century was an outcome of the cumulative development of pastoral labour in which ecology only played an indirect role. The Rift Valley and its environs has been home to a number of communities whose means of survival included hunting and gathering among the Ogiek, crop cultivation among the Agikuyu, and mixed farming among the Kalenjin and sections of the Maasai such as the Ilparakuyu. All these communities were occasionally forced by circumstances to adopt any of these activities as predominant means of survival. It would appear, therefore, that ecology did not play a primary role in the development of pastoralism among the Maasai. But once they adopted livestock keeping as an activity, they were simultaneously able to develop and organize their labour, social

5

institutions and beliefs around cattle. In the course of time, Maasai practices such as keeping of large herds of livestock and the burning of pasture, produced the pastoral ecology characterized by the steppe grassland and abundant animal life.

They also created specific pastoral relations of production which operated at the level of the domestic group, the local community (*enkutoto*) and the territorial sections (*iloshon*, singular; *olosho*). The domestic group was the primary unit of production and reproduction of both livestock and people. It consisted of the male owner of the homestead and his wives, children and other dependants. It controlled and appropriated to itself the major means of production, namely, the herd and the labour of its members, particularly that of the youth and women. In the established division of labour, young boys (*il ayiok*) and client herdsmen tended livestock, the young men (*il moran*) assisted in herd movement to pastures away from the homestead while women were primarily in charge of the production and distribution of food, mainly milk. The male head of the homestead controlled all the livestock which he distributed to his wives to hold in trust for their sons. Each domestic group could not survive on its own and was, therefore, linked to others through kinship and age-set ties. It was the necessity of this linkage that brought about the territorial level of pastoral production.

The territorial sections (*iloshon*) formed the communal production and political units that cut across both descent and age-set ties. Domestic groups within these sections possessed collective rights of appropriation of pasture, water and saltlicks.[10] They also appropriated the collective labour of the junior warriors who provided defence to resources of each section. It was at the territorial level that socio-economic differentiation took place. It was at this level that elders appropriated the labour of the junior warriors whose main functions included standing guard over livestock and providing defence. As a result of their differential access to pastoral resources, there emerged

6

the rich (*il karsisi*) and the poor (il *aisinak*). The rich elders became the political and ritual leaders in the sections that emerged.

During Olonana's youth, the following *iloshon* had emerged among the Maasai: Iloitokitoki, Ilaikipiak, Ildalat-le-kutuk, Ildamat, Ilkaputiei, Ilkekonyokie, Ilmatapato, Iloita, Iloodo-Kilani, Ilaitayoik, Ilpurko, Ilsikirari, Siria, Ilwuas Nkishu, Ilmoitanik, Ilkisongo, and Ilparakuyu. These sections had emerged partly as a result of the processes of incorporation and territorial expansion of original groups and their eventual fission as they became too large to cater for the needs of their constituent domestic units. These processes were partly attempts to resolve conflicts that emerged as a result of contradictions between the domestic and territorial relations of production. While each domestic unit aimed at autonomous appropriation of pastoral resources, the focus on territorial units was equal access to collectively exploited resources. It was usually impossible, in reality, to maintain a balance between the needs of the two units perpetually, except ideologically, through the invocation of descent, kinship and age-set ties. But these ideological constructs had their limitations and so domestic groups and communities broke and multiplied. At times they regrouped and formed alliances against each other. These processes can be said to have reached a peak in the nineteenth century, occasioning the civil wars. Another major problem with pastoralism as a system of production was the susceptibility of cattle to plague and drought. Olonana witnessed some of the civil wars during his youth. He was later engaged in war against his brother in the course of his ascendancy to power. He also witnessed major plagues in the 1880s and early 1890s.

Raids and civil wars were aspects of Maasai pastoral life that have been stereotyped. They have simply been explained in terms of the bloodthirstiness and warlike nature of the Maasai by European travellers like Joseph Thompson, christian missionaries and colonial administrators and some scholars. To all these people, what the Maasai needed was christianization, westernization and pacification through British colonization. Aspects of Maasai pastoralism such as the keeping of large numbers of livestock, sacrifices and rituals which involved slaughter of some livestock, and the movements of the Maasai with their stock, were deprecated and meant to be brought to an end. Even though these practices served a useful purpose as far as the Maasai were concerned, the colonial and post colonial agents of capitalist development desired and even attempted to abolish them without providing other viable alternatives. Colonial authorities would also be quite uncomfortable with Maasai institutions such as the *Laibon* and the age-grade and age-set systems. During the early years of colonialism, one of the major challenges that Olonana faced was the argument by the colonial authorities that Maasai pastoralism and its associated political institutions, were not only primitive but also economically worthless and inimical to law and order.

The *Laibon* institution

According to Peter Rigby[11] the incorporation and development of the *laibon* institution was brought about by contradictions and instability that developed within Maasailand following the penetration of the East African interior by merchant capital since the seventeenth century. This penetration led to the partial commoditization and unequal accumulation of livestock at the domestic level. This, in turn, led to greater competition for resources essential for the sustenance of the pastoral economy such as grazing land, sources of water, salt licks and labour. For the majority of the people, socio-economic reproduction became increasingly difficult as years wore on. The situation dramatically worsened in the nineteenth century, thereby precipitating civil wars among the different sections of the Maasai in the nineteenth century. The position of the *Laibon* assumed greater significance as he was now expected to perform prophetic and ritualistic roles.

The *Laibon's* new function specifically included warnings about unfavourable future events such as natural calamities and war. He was also expected to proffer correct advice on how people should respond. He mobilized coalitions during wartime and offered ritual blessings to warriors about to engage in war or raids. Furthermore, he gave advice to initiates during the major age-set rituals like *eunoto* by which junior warriors became senior warriors, and *olngesher* by which senior warriors attained the status of junior elders. Finally, he interpreted omens and used his power to counteract sorcery. As a consequence, prophets were widely sought to perform these functions. The activities of Olonana's grandfather Supet, and his father, Mbatian, between the 1820s and 1870s were, therefore, manifestations of changes in the positions and roles of the prophets. These two Maasai leaders are remembered for the success with which they steered the Ilpurko and Ilkisongo sections of the Maasai through bad times.

It was this socio-political ferment that led to the settlement of Olonana's forebears as a distinct community among the Ilkisongo at Ngosua near Monduli. This was an area a little to the south of Mt. Kilimanjaro. It was quite strategic as it was endowed with ample grazing land and water. Major trading routes passed close by, enabling the family of prophets to exchange both goods and ideas with merchants who often travelled from distant lands. It was here that Supet and Mbatian established and defined their role as war leaders, accumulated large herds of cattle, acquired many wives and raised large families. It was also here that Olonana was born and brought up before the family moved to Namanga.

By the nineteenth century, the *laibon* had thus become an integral part of the Maasai social formation, performing functions that were vital among the Maasai. They had established networks of relationships through marriage and had also been integrated into the Maasai age organization. They had become "insiders". Yet for some reason they remained "outsiders". Among the reasons for the latter dispensation was, first, due to their alien origin and adoption which were never lost to the ordinary Maasai. Secondly, they sometimes operated outside the moral and social boundaries of the Maasai community. For instance, apart from their normal share of war booty and other raided cattle, the prophets occasionally extorted from people large herds of livestock and appropriated wives without transfer of bridewealth. This was contrary to the very strict rules which regulated the acquisition and ownership of cattle and marriage among the Maasai. Furthermore, their relations with other institutions in the community such as the age-grade and age-set systems and their leaders were competitive and, therefore, conflictual. For instance, it was not always easy to establish a distinction between the prophets' essentially religious and ritual powers and the secular authority of the age-grade and age-set leaders. This often resulted in tension between the prophets and both the elders and warriors. The situation was complicated by the fact that, as certain sections of the Maasai community acquired their own prophets, there ensued very bitter competition between the prophets themselves and, of course, their followers.

The position of the prophets was, therefore, relatively delicate and limited as they had to balance and even neutralize many forces. Foremost in their strategy of survival was the establishment of an alliance with warriors. But even this has its own complication for members of this age-grade were divided into junior and senior groups. This posed the problem regarding the group of warriors with whom a prophet was likely to establish an alliance. Such alliance would be at the expense of one group of warriors and, of course, elders. Olonana would be faced with such difficult choices during struggles with his brother Senteu for leadership and ascendancy to *laibonship*. Among other things, he would ally himself with warriors, particularly those from his own age-set.

The age-grade and age-set systems

Both the age-grade and the age-set systems, referred to as *olporror*, existed among the Maasai long before the rise of the institution of *laibon*. But since the seventeenth century, the dynamics of the age-set system became linked to the influence and power of the great prophets.

Both systems were elaborately structured to play very vital roles among the Maasai. Age-grades were, and still are, "the successive statuses to which individuals are ascribed in the course of their lives."[12] One was allocated specific tasks, functions, authority and influence on the basis of one's age-grade. For, instance, the uncircumcised youth, *laiyok*, tended calves, sheep and goats near the homestead but had no status in the public domain. After their circumcision, *emurata*, and after the first meat-eating ceremony, *olpul*, the *laiyok* would occupy the status of warriors, *moran*. But they would first be junior warriors until after another major ceremony, *eunoto*, about ten years later. This ceremony made them senior warriors.

The *moran* were a reserve army whose main duties included defence of the community against external aggression, maintenance of internal law and order, and the execution of military raids for purposes of territorial expansion and accumulation of livestock. The *moran* were expected to respect elders who determined when they married and when they became elders. This was a factor that often created tension between the *moran* and the elders. But the *moran* always looked forward to the *olngesher*. After this ceremony they now exercised secular power and authority and, with the passage of time, they became senior elders, *intsati*, who were the custodians of Maasai history, law and culture.

The age-grade system only organized the Maasai society occupationally and hierarchically during an individual's lifetime, but the age-set system did so temporally and spatially. It also conferred permanent status on individuals. A new age-set was formed once every fifteen years and comprised "all those within a broad range of ages who are formed into a group of peers with their own separate identity."[13] Members of the same age-set referred to themselves as *olaji*. Only men became members of the respective age-sets after *olngesher* ceremony. Upon their marriage, women automatically became members of their husbands' age-sets.

The age systems operated alongside the kinship system to provide the institutional framework for socio-political integration and the mobilization of human and economic resources. First, it placed individuals spatially and temporally and in specific relationships with others in society. In so doing, it enabled them to develop a sense of being Maasai, a process that continued throughout one's life. In this regard, the age-systems were integrative because of their extra-territorial orientation and ideology. Through such memorable events like circumcision, and transitional ceremonies like *olpul, eunoto* and *olngesher*, the age-systems were a source of the community's history and heritage and served this purpose more effectively than the kin-based genealogical reckoning, whose depth never exceeded three generations. This is not to minimize the role clan legends played. They also linked the young and old members of the community in relations of political authority and affinity and helped in the recruitment of political leaders. Further, it provided an effective means for military mobilization. As John Galaty puts it: "The Maasai age-system offered a framework for social and military aggregation whereby significant massing could occur across age and territory, space and time, creating a potent force out of a widely dispersed population."[14] Last but not least, the age-grade and the kinship systems also functioned as relations of production since they were used to determine access to resources that were essential for the development of the agro-pastoral economy, namely, grazing land and water. They also aided in the distribution of pastoral products such as livestock, meat ,milk and butter. As ideology, they were a means by which the following virtues were inculcated: egalitarianism, selfhood, ethics and morality, familyhood, honour and bravery. It was into a society that cherished these ideals that Olonana was socialized.

Olonana's initiation and apprenticeship

Olonana participated in the important ceremonies by which individuals in the Maasai community were initiated into age-grades and age-sets. He was circumcised in 1882 and later initiated into the *Il Talala* age-set. Olonana, together with his peers, valued and looked forward to circumcision with open restlessness. Their circumcision had been delayed for some considerable time by Mbatian and the elders because of the Iloikop wars. When the long awaited moment finally came, the traditional sequence of events followed, closely supervised by elders and the young boys' patrons. Olonana participated in the initial four-day dance and ritual in a home he, together with other youth, had constructed for this purpose. A bull was slaughtered for the feast. The boys selected their spokesman, the *olaiguenani*, from among themselves. This marked the first stage of the initiation process and a worthy training in collective merry-making and leadership.

The second stage came after a while. Olonana and his peers came together again. This time, using their bare hands, they wrestled and knocked down a strong bullock. They also selected from among themselves a boy whose bull would be slaughtered for the feast. The boy subsequently became the ceremonial leader of the impending circumcision, the *Olopolosi olkiteng*. Again this signified collective strength and decision-making that would be demanded of them as the prospective warrior age-group.

Finally, there was the actual circumcision. Olonana and Mbatian's other sons went through the ordeal in their home as did other boys. The operation lasted about five minutes during which the initiate was not expected to flinch in any way. It was the moment for demonstrating one's manhood. Like most other boys, Olonana tried, as much as he could, neither to hold the circumciser's hands nor to twitch any part of his body. He sat still, staring fixedly ahead, until the circumciser completed his task. He hated to be considered a cowardly flincher, an *olkaasiode*. Like the rest of the boys, Olonana then spent a few days in his mother's house to heal. After some months he became a full *moran*, a most coveted position among the Maasai.

After his circumcision, Olonana now enjoyed the privilege of a *moran*. He could now dance and flirt with girls. He joined his warrior age-mates in their newly established villages, the *imanyat*, and in cattle raids. Generally, he interacted with them as members of the same age-grade. He now wore the *moran* hair-style and other regalia which symbolized his position as a son of a prophet, an *inkidong*. For Olonana, the rituals associated with initiation into warriorhood were moments of shared learning, endurance, feasting and other experiences. Members of Olonana's age-grade would soon form the *Il Talala* age-set.

But unlike his age-mates, Olonana was also apprenticed as an *inkidongi*. Despite the belief among the Maasai that the gift and power of prophecy is inherited patrilineally, descendants of the *laibon* had to learn the trade. In this regard, Olonana was relatively disadvantaged by the fact that Mbatian preferred to show his favourite son, Senteu, the intricacies of prophetic practice. He would also allow Senteu to deal with some of his clients to gain practical knowledge and influence. Mbatian was preparing Senteu to succeed him. It would be right to suggest that since Olonana knew he was a potential prophet by birth, he was determined to learn the art by other means. He probably did so through other practitioners, namely, his uncles and cousins more than by occasionally observing what his father did to clients. In time, Olonana himself had a number of clients among his own age-mates whose warrior villages he visited frequently. He travelled to many parts of Maasailand, learning and practising. In 1889, Olonana was encountered near Naivasha by two European travellers, Jackson and Gedge, most probably in one of his many healing sojourns in Maasailand.

The civil wars

The other major events that occurred during Olonana's youth were the Maasai civil wars. These wars, better known as *iloikop* wars, started in the 1830s and continued well into the 1880s. They were fought in three stages: the Iloogolala war 1830-40; the Iloosekelai war 1840s; and the Ilaikipak war 1860-1880s. Among the most serious misinterpretations of the causes of these wars are the ones proffered by D. A. Low who erroneously states that the wars were caused by "the more general equilibrium which had overtaken the region as a whole and by the fact that the "warlike Maasai" (a people so addicted to the practice of warfare) turned upon each other for lack of anyone else of substance to fight."[15] He adds that some of these wars were "in the nature of jousts and tournaments". Low's explanation for the wars is that the Maasai were engaged in them because they were by nature "warlike" and that having looked around for non-existent enemies, they turned against each other. This is really not a valid explanation since its portrayal of the Maasai is not even in accord with the peaceful nature of the people who are known to fight only when provoked by "enemies" or by circumstances.

In this particular case the enemies and the circumstances were "internal" to the Maasai community. The civil conflicts were abetted by internal and external factors. Essentially, the Maasai civil wars were caused by the contradictions inherent within pastoral accumulation and reproduction at the level of the territorial relations of production. As has already been explained regarding pastoral production, households within the territorial sections usually competed for access to pastoral resources. This, in turn, ultimately forced each of the territorial sections to expand. This was done at the expense of other sections who were bound to fight in defence of their territorial integrity.

Three factors worsened the situation in the nineteenth century. One was the expansion of new agricultural communities, mostly the Agikuyu, Akamba, Nandi and Kipsigis, who settled along either side of the Rift Valley between the eighteenth and nineteenth centuries, an event which blocked outward Maasai expansion and forced them to fight against each other. Secondly, the advancement of European and Arab imperialism also increased competition for resources. Finally, the advent of widespread drought sparked off the initial conflict in southern Maasailand towards the end of the 1830s, thus starting the chain of events that were to continue almost throughout the rest of the nineteenth century.

The *Ilaikipiak* war of 1860-80s was fought during Olonana's youth. The war was initially sparked off by Ilaikipiak expansionist activities against the Ilpurko in the area around Nakuru and Naivasha. According to Maasai tradition, as recorded by John Berntsen, the incident that precipitated the conflict was disagreement between the Ilpurko and Ilaikipiak over the spoils of a raid they had jointly undertaken against Ilwuas Nkishu.[16] The Ilpurko are said to have taken more than their share of the raided cattle, an act that prompted the Ilaikipiak under the leadership of their *laibon*, Koikoti ole Tunai, to retaliate.

Although Koikoti was actually Mbatian's nephew, since his mother Nanetia was the latter's sister, he was determined to challenge his uncle. To make his point, Koikoti taunted Mbatian, who was *laibon* of the Ilpurko and other Maasai sections as well. "Mbatian", Koikoti chanted, "You are like a fake, you are not circumcised; your penis is full of dung."[17] Through this taunt, Koikoti had not only questioned Mbatian's manhood but also his position as the foremost *laibon*.

Thus, challenged, Mbatian was determined to defend his position and to prove to his nephew that he was more powerful by defeating his followers but sparing him. "Koikoti, my nephew," said Mbatian, "I will not kill you since I do not want my sister to cry for me, but I will ensure that you have no place to settle. I will block the sun and the moon so that you tread in the dark."[18] Mbatian soon formed a military coalition consisting of the Ilpurko, Ilkisongo, Iloitai, Ilkaputei and Ildamat to fight the Ilaikipiak. He is said to have further used his magical powers so effectively that when his coalition forces met the Koikoti's Ilaikipiak, the latter were utterly defeated. A big number were killed while many more lost their livestock and were dispatched helter-skelter, abandoning their lands that had once stretched from Naivasha to the Leroghi plateau. Koikoti himself fled to live among the Isaria in the Trans-Mara region while the remnants of his followers moved further north to organize rearguard raids against the Samburu, Rendille and Borana. Other Ilaikipiak took refuge among the Agikuyu and Ameru and were gradually absorbed by these communities. The more unfortunate ones became Iltorobo, having reverted to hunting and gathering after losing all their livestock and the ability to rebuild new stock.

The Ilaikipiak war was fought most bitterly between 1874 and 1875. Thereafter, raids continued among the Maasai but on a smaller scale and more sporadically throughout the 1880s. During these years Olonana was too young to participate in the Ikoikop war. But like other children in Mbatian's kraal at Monduli and its neighbourhood, he was affected by the turmoil. People lived in fear and were unable to engage in all the normal activities. It is possible that Olonana and his peers were circumstantially forced to spend more time herding livestock around the safety of their fathers' homesteads when warriors and clients who should have taken them further afield were engaged in fighting. It is possible that moments of joy, such as when children play, tell stories and ape activities of older people, were rudely interrupted by war cries meant to alert people about actual attacks by or against the enemy. But the war also had a positive consequence. It provided an opportunity for Mbatian to bring together different Maasai sections in an alliance or coalition whose core were the Ilpurko. In fact, after the defeat of the Ilaikipiak, the Ilpurko occupied a pre-eminent position throughout the rest of Mbatian's life. In later years this would constitute Olonana's territorial inheritance.

In 1889, at about the age of nineteen, Olonana had become a product of the times. He had grown up during the period of turbulence brought about by war and disease. These events transformed certain aspects of Maasai pastoral economy, culture and political institutions. Yet this was also a period of continuity as most aspects of Maasai economy and society persisted. Olonana, therefore, symbolized change and continuity among the Maasai. He was initiated into the age-grade system that provided the rhythm of life within the community. The age-grade system positioned him temporarilly while birth and apprenticeship within the *Laibon* family equipped him with the ability and skills to "see", explain and resolve the challenges that faced members of the community. The following year the most immediate challenge pitted him against his own brother, Senteu. It was the struggle for succession to the highest and most enviable position that was occupied by his ailing father, Mbatian.

Chapter Two

Olonana's Ascendancy: 1890-1898

A number of events occurred between 1890 and 1898 which determined Olonana's destiny. These included the death of his father Mbatian and the war that ensued between Olonana and Senteu. Drought and disease had ravaged Maasailand. Thirdly, there was the coming of the British, represented at the time by the Imperial British East African Company under Francis Hall. This chapter analyses the manner in which Olonana responded to these events which were crucial to his rise to power.

Mbatian's death and the legends about his succession

Towards the end of the 1880s, the Maasai, the Inkidongi in particular, had every reason to be anxious. Olonana's father, Mbatian, was senile, blind and quite sickly. There was talk that Mbatian's cousin, Makoo, had bewitched the old prophet and was responsible for his ailment. This suspicion was part of Maasai tradition regarding their prophets. None of them died through a natural cause. As days passed and Mbatian showed no signs of recovery, most people were convinced that the prophet would eventually die. Their main worry was that he had taken too long to name his successor. His sons, Olonana and Senteu, were waiting anxiously, each one hoping he would succeed his father. Some members of the Inkidongi were already prepared to support Senteu; others were quietly assuring Olonana of their backing in the event of Mbatian's death. Mbatian died in 1890 and a succession war ensued between the two rivals.

The immediate turn of events is contained in two legends narrated by S. S. Ole Sankan and Sydney Langford Hinde, respectively. Sankan's narrative is as follows:

> When he (Mbatian) realized that his end was near, he called Senteu, his eldest and favourite son, so that he might bequeath to him the secrets of the art. He said, "My son, I am about to die and would like to leave my powers with

you. So, please get up very early in the morning before anyone else is awake and come to my bed so that nobody else may hear what I am going to tell you. You will become a powerful leader of all my people, and no one will ever supersede you." All this was said while Olonana was concealed in the calf pen inside the house, and he therefore heard everything, including the things that Senteu was asked to bring with him.

Olonana immediately went to his mother and told her what was going to happen. The two conspired and decided that Olonana was going to impersonate Senteu and receive the power and blessings. They both knew that Mbatian was senile and would not be able to tell the difference between his two sons. Olonana's mother rationalized that both Senteu and Olonana were equally Mbatian's sons and the act was therefore justified. Olonana got up in the small hours of the morning and went to his father. His father asked, "Who are you?" and Olonana immediately said, "Father, I am your son Senteu." After the old man had imparted everything to him he said, "My son come close to me so that I embrace you and put you close to my chest." After that Mbatian said, "Now kiss this tongue." When this was over he was asked to leave immediately before anyone else came. He had received all the authority from his father.

On his way out of the house he met Senteu at the door. But they did not even exchange greetings. The father heard Senteu coming in and asked who it was. When Senteu replied, his father recognized the voice and asked who it was that had been there before him. Senteu said that he had met his younger half brother at the door and was told what had happened. "What was more", he was told, "What is done cannot be undone especially as you are both my children." The only thing that was given, therefore, was a magical box with which he could curse and cast spells on people, and he was told that his family would multiply. But that he had to accept Olonana as his superior in other fields.[1]

The foregoing legend has many significations. First, it is likely that although Mbatian had wished to name Senteu his successor, he never publicly did so before his death and his choice of Senteu in the privacy of his deathbed was simply overridden. Olonana, knowing that he was not his father's favourite son, went ahead and pronounced himself the *Laibon*. The legend, therefore, confirms the traditional problem of succession to *laibonship* among the Maasai. It is likely that there was no fixed regulation governing succession and that the position was usually open to any one of the incumbent's sons so long as he was a member of the warrior age-set. This implies that although the position was hereditary, the sons were expected to struggle for it.

The second significance of the legend is its moral lesson expressed in the following Maasai proverb: "The son of the beloved wife could be advised but that of the unloved wife may heed the advice," (*Eikoki olenkirotel nening olentinki*).[2] Olonana succeeded Mbatian because, unlike Senteu his more favoured rival, he listened to advice and acted promptly. Thirdly, the legend was intended to provide an explanation to what had already happened in order to rationalize and even legitimize Olonana's position. In the process, Senteu was relegated to lower position.

Around 1899 Hinde, a colonial administrator, recorded another legend about Olonana's accession to power. Like the legend above, Hinde's story favours Olonana and is obviously intended to legitimize Olonana's position as *laibon* and colonial chief. According to this legend, Mbatian had, long before his death, decided that Olonana must succeed him since Senteu "had from his boyhood been both quarrelsome and deceitful."[3] Hinde's story contradicts itself by stating that before Mbatian's death, he gave Senteu and Olonana an opportunity to prove themselves. "He placed all his medicine into a living tree and proclaimed that whichever of his two sons found and appropriated it should be his successor."[4] In the search that ensued, Olonana found the medicine and this was looked at by the Maasai as evidence of his fitness to succeed his father in chieftainship."[5]

Soon afterwards Mbatian called elders and warriors to witness Olonana's installation. Hinde describes the occasion as follows:

> The ceremony of investing Lenana with the royal succession was accordingly held. Mbatian took off his right sandal and put it on Lenana's right foot to show that Lenana would follow in his footsteps. Then he unbuckled his sword and placed it in Lenana's right hand, indicating that his battles would be Lenana's. He also took a strip of skin garment he was wearing and fastened it round Lenana's neck, as a symbol that his possessions were made over to Lenana. Finally, the royal medicine was handed over, thus completing the ceremony.[6]

According to Hinde's story, therefore, Olonana succeeded his father Mbatian because he was more intelligent than Senteu and possessed good leadership qualities. Furthermore, Olonana's installation as Maasai leader was a public function attended by both elders and warriors. This is in contrast to the other legend in which Mbatian bestowed Olonana with prophetic powers in his deathbed.

It is not surprising that Hinde's version of Mbatian's succession favoured Olonana. As explained later in this chapter, colonial administrators were determined to build up Olonana by justifying his accession to power. It would really be interesting to know the version offered by Senteu's followers and sympathizers.

Times of trouble: disease, drought and war

Olonana's rise to power and the concomitant war between himself and Senteu, must also be analyzed within the broader context of the other events that occurred at the time: epidemics, drought, famine, intersectional wars and European intervention. Mbatian is said to have prophesied these events, and to have particularly warned the Maasai against fighting the Europeans. The total eclipse of the sun in September 1889, a few months before the prophet's own demise, only lent mystical credence to the portents of the time and underlined the significance of the events themselves.

The cattle epidemics, *Bovine pleuro-pneumonia* (*ol kipie*), had broken out much earlier in 1883. The disease had its own long history. Its origins were outside Africa. It appeared in South Africa in the 1850s and Chad in the late 1870s, and spread to Eastern Africa in the 1880s. The first Maasai cattle to be affected by the epidemic were those of the Ilpurko which contracted the disease from the already infected ones captured in raids by Ilpurko warriors. Ilpurko herds then spread the disease among others. The epidemic reappeared in June 1897. Another cattle epidemic, rinderpest (*olodua*), broke out in 1890-91 and a second time in 1898-1900. Its origins were also extraneous. Cattle belonging to the Ilkisongo were the first to be affected but the disease soon spread to the Naivasha area. Laikipia and Samburu herds affected those of the Purko.

The droughts of 1884-6 and 1897 and the epidemics, referred to by the Maasai as *emutai* or *enkidaaroto*, killed thousands of Maasai cattle. Olonana lost almost one thousand head of cattle in 1897, due to *pleuro-pneumonia* and a large herd in 1899 following the second rinderpest epidemic. Smallpox (*entidiae*) broke out in 1892 and again in 1899 to claim a large number of people. When famine hit Maasailand between 1898 and 1899, it found people who had suffered from loss of cattle and weakened by smallpox. Both the Maasai and their herds were reduced to half their previous numbers. The lasting impact of these natural disasters was to pit the Maasai sections against one another in wars, popularly known as *morijo*.

The primary purpose of these wars was to recover lost stock. Struggles for grazing grounds were a secondary cause of these wars. This situation was necessitated by an imbalance the epidemics created in different areas regarding numbers of livestock and human population.

Richard Waller has convincingly explained how the differential effects of the epidemics led to a situation whereby "an imbalance appeared between those groups which still had livestock but too few people to manage it adequately and those who had lost their stock but not their people. This provided a tempting opportunity for the *moran,* who desperately needed to find stock to feed their families to guarantee their own future."[7] Due to the environmental crisis, the *moran* required the *Laibon* to bless the cattle raids that they organized, and to protect the livestock already in their possession and heal the sick ones. The situation explains the inter-sectional conflicts among the Maasai at the time and the contest between Olonana and Senteu.

War between Olonana and Senteu

The rivalry between Olonana and Senteu was, therefore, not simply personal. It reflected the rivalry between the two main Maasai sections, the Ilpurko led by Olonana, and the Ilotai, who recognized Senteu as their *laibon.* Alan Jacobs has argued further that at another level, the struggles between the two brothers reflected the wider conflict between senior warriors and junior elders.[8] Jacobs does not explain why Olonana led only the Ilpurko while Senteu championed the interests of Ilotai junior elders.

Olonana and Senteu fought at a time when European powers, Britain and Germany were also struggling to occupy their spheres of influence in East Africa. This was quite significant. As Waller has argued, "the contrast in the pattern of relations which developed between the British and the Ilpurko, on the one hand, and between the Germans and the Iloitai, on the other, were decisive in determining the outcome of the civil war."[9] Whereas Olonana and his Ilpurko followers were able to establish an alliance with British agents, Senteu and his Ilotai supporters were never able to come to friendly terms with the Germans. It was primarily Olonana's ability to capitalize on this situation that, in the final analysis, led to his triumph over Senteu and his ascendancy to power as an *Oloibon* and colonial paramount chief.

After Mbatian's death in 1890, Olonana and Senteu moved from the Namanga area to settle in different places. While Olonana and his cousin Ngaroya settled around Naivasha, Senteu went to live close to Loita hills. During the initial stages of their conflict, Senteu was better placed than Olonana. He enjoyed more traditional support and his Iloita warriors were involved in more rewarding raids than the Ilpurko. For instance, in late 1893, the Iloitai with their allies, the Ilkisongo, Illsikirari, and Ilarusha attacked, defeated and absorbed the Siria, Laitayok and Salei. They also attacked the Ilmatapato, Ilkaputiei and other Maasai close to Nairobi. In contrast, the Ilpurko with their only ally the Ilkekonyukie attacked the Ildamat and Ildalalekutuk. In 1894 Senteu's warriors successfully attacked Olonana and his followers and took away large numbers of livestock. Olonana also faced raids from the Agikuyu in the course of 1894 and afterwards.

Olonana establishes relation with Francis Hall

The pressure of the Iloita and Gikuyu attacks forced Olonana to intensify his request to Francis Hall, an agent of the Imperial British East Africa Company already stationed in Fort Smith (now Kabete), for protection. Relations between Olonana and Hall had actually commenced in 1893.[10] While Olonana's decision to initiate relations with the British were influenced by his own personal interests and what he perceived to be those of the Maasai sections he led, Hall, on the other hand, desired to use Olonana and the Maasai to further British imperialism. From the outset, therefore, Maasai and British interests, represented by Olonana and Hall, respectively, were not compatible.

First and foremost, Olonana wanted Hall to provide him with military help against Senteu and the Iloita. This consideration coincided with the Ilkaputiei, Ilmatapato and Ilpurko desire for protection against the Iloita and Ilarusha. Secondly, Olonana considered the possibility of the British granting asylum to those of his followers who were refugees: victims of disease and war. Thirdly, Olonana's followers who had been dispersed by war and disease hoped that, apart from providing them with protection, an alliance with the British would enable them to regroup and build up new stock. This again coincided with Olonana's own ambition to use the British to accumulate more stock, having lost hundreds of cattle. Like his father, Olonana hoped to acquire large herds of cattle with the help of the *moran*. The British would help his own *moran* launch raids through which he would get his own traditional share as *laibon*. He wanted stock to marry more wives, as he had only one at the time. He also wanted to enhance his own political position through dispensation of patronage in the form of cattle to his followers and his clients. British support would also enable him to arbitrate in disputes among his people and between them and their neighbours. It is important to note that the British would not support all of Olonana's demands. They assessed their relations with Olonana on the basis of their own interests.

Security was foremost among Hall's considerations regarding the advancement of British imperialism. Olonana's Maasai inhabited an area through which caravans passed on their way to Uganda and, incidentally, a route through which the Mombasa-Kisumu railway, under construction at the time, would pass. It was necessary that members of the caravan pass safely and those building the railway proceed uninterrupted. It was also necessary that they be provisioned with meat and other necessities. It was essential for the government to establish peaceful relations with the Maasai to ensure the security of both the caravan and the railway. The British had never completely changed their earlier attitude that the Maasai were "warlike" and intractable even though the latter had been seriously weakened by disease and inter-sectional wars. An alliance with them meant placing a potentially dangerous enemy on their side. The British also believed that the Maasai were fine soldiers, thanks to the stereotype about their warriors. The British also wanted a local militia that was cheap, efficient and controllable. They believed that the Maasai warriors possessed these attributes. Such a force would be mobilized against people such as sections of the Agikuyu and Nandi, who persistently resisted British colonization. Finally, the British considered the fact that to establish an effective alliance with the Maasai, they required a local leader through whom they could effectively communicate with the rest of the community. Hall believed that Olonana was just the type of Maasai leader they needed. He already had claims to the highest position among the Maasai and, therefore, possessed authority, was also amenable and could be manipulated. Besides, Olonana lived much closer to the British post at Fort Smith than Senteu did. It must be pointed out that despite their alliance with Olonana and the Maasai, the British and their local agents would treat the latter with a lot of suspicion and caution. This was largely because the ultimate interests of the parties involved were in diametrical opposition to each other. The British, therefore, supported Olonana's interests very selectively and to the extent that this did not contradict their own scheme as the following instances illustrate.

At Fort Smith, Hall had established trading relations with the Maasai. He also used Maasai warriors against the neighbouring Agikuyu, a factor that really strained relations between the two communities. This had forced Olonana to invite Hall and six Gikuyu elders to his kraal in October, 1893. He had hoped that Hall would reconcile the two warring communities. Hall reported as follows about the meeting:

> It was decided that I was to go with six headmen, and see the Maasai Chief... I took 20 picked men in case of accidents and we had a very jolly walk through the forest by-paths for about three hours to the head kraal, and here I took my seat under a shady tree and waited. After some time a chief and the general of the elmoran came out... then we got to business. It was a most funny day altogether. Sometimes when I was sitting down one would come up, shake hands and then take off my hat, shake my hair, pull my beard, pass their hand over my face and then examine my hat, clothes, boots, and everything... My men simply rolled about in laughter.[11]

It is clear from this statement that Hall was suspicious of the Maasai who reacted to the white man's presence with open curiosity. With Olonana's initiative, Hall tried to reconcile the two communities.

A truce followed but was quickly brought to an end by the fact that shortly later, the Agikuyu lured a few Maasais into their villages and murdered them at night. Hall retaliated by mobilizing Olonana's Maasai warriors against them. They killed six and wounded five Agikuyu and confiscated about one hundred goats from the suspected culprits. This was not strange as Hall always played the two communities against each other. He was also reputed for meting out excessive punishment to offenders.

In January 1894, Olonana also paid Hall a visit at the station. The purpose of the visit was to request Hall to assist him against Senteu and to give refuge to his people who had been displaced by disease and war. Hall refused the first request but granted the second one. Initially about thirty Maasai women and children settled at the station. By June, more refugees joined, dramatically increasing their number to one thousand men, women and children. These were far beyond the station's capacity. Besides, Kinyanjui, the local Agikuyu leader, expressed his people's apprehension about the large number of Maasai in their midst. Hall decided to resettle them at Ngong. He moved them in groups under armed escort. A party of Agikuyu warriors waited until Hall's armed escort withdrew. They then set upon the first group of Maasai refugees, butchered male Maasai and abducted women and children. When Hall received the bad news he ordered the Gikuyu to return those abducted and that they pay a fine of one hundred goats. Hall continued to use Maasai warriors against The Agikuyu, paying them with captured stock. This ingratiated him to the Maasai but resulted in increased antipathy between the Maasai and the Agikuyu. Eventually, the entire Maasai refugee groups were settled at Ngong. This boosted Olonana's position as he had negotiated the exercise. But the Maasai paid a price with their lives. Their relations with the Agikuyu deteriorated considerably.

Renewed hostilities between Olonana and Senteu

Senteu and the Iloita renewed their attacks against Olonana during the early months of 1895. Olonana was, once more, forced to request for British protection, permission and support to send retaliatory raids against his adversary. The British accepted the first request but found it impossible to aid Olonana's retaliatory raids against the Iloita. It was easy for the British to protect Olonana from within their side of the boundary between the East Africa Protectorate and German East Africa. The British were reluctant to support Olonana's raids against Senteu since they entailed entry into German territory. But to keep him happy, they told him they would not stop him from carrying out these raids. Of course, the British were sure that the Germans on the other side of the border would know how to deal with the situation. There were times when both the British and the Germans considered the fight between Olonana and Senteu to be in their interest as this gave them time to deal with African communities and to establish effective administration.

On 1 July, 1895, the British government decided to formally take over the Imperial British East Africa Company, the stretch of country between Uganda Protectorate and Mombasa. The area became known as the East Africa Protectorate, a name that is used in this book because of its historical significance, instead of Kenya as the country came to be renamed in 1920. The boundary between the two countries was drawn just west of Olonana's kraal at Ngong. It divided the Maasai between two countries. Those in Uganda Protectorate were administered from Naivasha, while the ones in the East Africa Protectorate were administered from Fort Smith with assistance from Ngong station, both of which were in Ukamba Province. Administrators in both countries took interest in Olonana and the Maasai even though the Maasai themselves neither knew nor were bothered by the fact that, at this time they were administratively under three foreign regimes. During the same year, the British approved the construction of the Uganda Railway from Mombasa to Lake Victoria. Since the railway was surveyed to pass through Maasailand, Olonana and the Maasai attained even greater strategic positions for the administrative officials in Uganda and the East Africa Protectorate.

The Kedong massacre and the Dick affair

Another incident which occurred in late December 1895, put to test the regard the British had for Olonana, the understanding between the Maasai and the British, and the strength of British administration. This was the Kedong massacre and the Dick affair which occurred when Hall was away in Britain on sick leave.[12] On 24th December, 1895, a large caravan of Agikuyu and Swahili porters had camped at Kedong Valley, close to Maasai homesteads. Later in the night, some of their *askaris* entered the homesteads uninvited and abducted two young girls to their camp, seemingly to assuage their sexual urge, much to the enragement of the Maasai *moran* who would have retaliated were it not for their elders' advice against it. The elders had told the *moran* to overlook the provocation since Olonana was, at the time, on a visit to Fort Smith. The *moran* spent the rest of the night trembling with pent up anger.

Early the next morning as the caravan set off, two things occurred that set the *moran*, who were still seething with anger, against the caravaneers. A noise from the caravan startled cattle; there was also an actual attempt to steal cattle. Women responded with screams and a frightened Swahili nervously discharged his gun, instantly killing a calf. A large number of armed *moran* who were on the alert set upon the enemy whose retreat and fire were belated and unco-ordinated. Very many of them were slaughtered but a few escaped to report the incident.

One of the people to be informed about the massacre by fleeing survivors was Andrew Dick, a British trader and former accountant of the Imperial British East Africa Company. Dick was on a trading expedition towards Lake Turkana. He vowed to avenge the massacre, perhaps to uphold British prestige or to use it as a pretext to loot Maasai cattle. He immediately requested for reinforcements from Fort Smith. Gilkinson, who was in charge of the fort at the time, dispatched an armed party with orders that Dick accompanies them to the fort. The trader ignored the order and, accompanied by his *askaris*, proceeded to Kedong Valley on 27th December. On arrival, Dick and his small army indiscriminately seized large numbers of cattle and shot at the herdsmen who dared to stop them. He killed about one hundred Maasai before being killed himself after his gun jammed. Six of his *askaris* were also killed by Maasai spearmen. The survivors in Dick's party made a quick retreat to Fort Smith but failed to retrieve their master's body. They took away the two hundred cattle and seventy five donkeys they had managed to loot from the Maasai.

Olonana, and five Maasai elders who had accompanied him to Fort Smith,were meanwhile detained for questioning. He was highly suspected by the British administrators at the Fort, of having either organized or approved of the massacre. Had he, therefore, visited the Fort to establish an alibi? Did he possess information that could lead to the arrest of the perpetrators of the dastardly act? Also present at the Fort at the time was Fredrick Jackson, an administrator of Uganda's Eastern Province which extended up to Naivasha at the time. John Ainsworth, who was trying to impose British authority over the Akamba to the north of Machakos, received information about the Kedong massacre and Dick's killing and hurried to the Fort. He immediately commenced investigations into the matter.

Ainsworth received more background information from Gilkinson. He also interrogated a few Maasai elders and *moran* from Kedong Valley to get their version of the story. On 29th December, accompanied by Gilkinson, he discussed the incident with Olonana and the five Maasai elders at the Fort. Ainsworth finally concluded that the Maasai had been seriously provoked by both the caravaneers and Dick and that the Maasai action was neither premeditated nor planned. His investigations led him to conclude that in both instances, the Maasai had acted in self-defence. Indeed, Ainsworth had earlier informed Arthur Hardinge, the Commissioner of the East Africa Protectorate, that:

> It appears that Lenana, the Chief of these Maasai was on very friendly terms with the Kikuyu station. At the time of the massacre he was actually on a visit to the Fort where

> he remains a friendly hostage. This fact leads me to think
> that the massacre has been an accident caused by the
> caravan marching past the kraals in the dark.[13]

Now that he had a clearer perspective of the incident, he completely exonerated the Maasai and, of course, Olonana from any blame. The way Ainsworth dealt with the situation was quite unique in comparison to how colonial officials reacted to almost similar situations in other parts of Kenya. Ordinarily, punitive measures would have been taken against the Maasai. Olonana and the five Maasai elders would have either been deported or killed. Yet neither of these things happened. Why?

One possible answer is that the British always feared a general uprising of the Maasai *moran* whose military strength they overestimated. The Kedong massacre only confirmed these fears. Secondly, Ainsworth thought that, in the next few days, the Maasai would most likely want to avenge Dick's behaviour, something that would result in a military encounter the British were not prepared for at the time. The route to Uganda would be blocked and the construction of the railway would be disrupted. Furthermore, any destruction of the Anglo-Maasai co-operation would imperil the advancements of British colonization in other parts of the country since the Maasai would withdraw their assistance. Ainsworth himself stated these fears in his diary, "I think we can fairly let the Maasai alone and make peace, the more so is this necessary for the fact that if we wished we could not take action against them. We, in our present position, are not strong enough."[14] It was clear that the British took cognizance of their own weakness and were anxious to make peace with the Maasai.

The way the British treated Olonana during the brief crisis, reflected this anxiety as well as the little regard British administrative officials had for him. That Olonana and the five Maasai elders who happened to have been visiting the Fort at the time of the massacre were held hostage there for close to five days, was indicative of the mistrust with which he was held by the administrative officials. Seemingly, Hall and Ainsworth simply tolerated him for his pivotal role in the Anglo-Maasai cooperation. In spite of Olonana's alleged shortcomings, the local British administrative agents still considered him an instrument of peace and a loyal mouthpiece of British policy. The role Olonana was expected to play would increasingly erode his own authority among his people.

On his release from "prison" at the Fort, Olonana was ordered to instruct the Maasai who had built homesteads close to the Uganda road to move away from the area. He was also requested to sanction the establishment of a government station at Naivasha and forbid stock raids. Although Olonana obediently obeyed and did as he was instructed by the Protectorate administration, the Maasai did not approve of these measures since they restricted their freedom and movements. The entrenchment of British authority circumscribed the freedom with which the Maasai wanted to further their pastoralist interests, including cattle raids which Olonana was expected to curtail to the chagrin of the *moran*. Olonana also risked his own position and authority among the Maasai.

But this was not the concern of the British so long as Olonana remained their loyal intermediary. "Had Olonana not been a strong man he is and a great friend of the European", Ainsworth informed Hardinge on 20 March, 1896, in obvious satisfaction with the turn of events, "nothing would have saved the situation after the Kedong massacre."[15] It is noteworthy that Olonana had also played a key role in the subsequent settlement with the aggrieved Agikuyu whose relatives had been killed by the Maasai during the Kedong incident. A special meeting had been held between five Maasai chiefs, Gikuyu elders, two European administrators, Fredrick Jackson and John Ainsworth and Olonana himself. The Gikuyu elders were convinced that the Maasai were not at fault. They were further appeased that the families of the Gikuyu porters who had been killed would be compensated. In subsequent years, Olonana was to be involved by the administrators in equally difficult negotiations.

The Maasai "scare" and Hardinge's talks with Olonana

In 1896, a *moran* leader, *ol aiguenani* Ole Kordilo, defiantly led a cattle raid across the border into German East Africa. The British reacted by confiscating the raided stock and exiling ole Kordilo. Ole Kordilo reacted by defiantly mobilizing other *moran* in Loitokitok to continue the raids. This heightened tension among themselves and between them and the colonial authorities. Hall, who had returned to the country in June, visited Olonana in November 1896 to work out ways and means of stopping the raids in order to ease these tensions. Little success was achieved as the raids continued.

The situation was worsened the following year by a combination of other events. The Germans across the border were determined to curtail Senteu's ability to effect raids. Senteu sent pleas to Olonana to join him in a united attack against both the British and the Germans. There ensued general restlessness among the Maasai, partly also, as a consequence of the decimation of their stock following the outbreak of *pleuro-pneumonia* in May 1897. It became necessary for the Maasai in East African Protectorate and German East Africa to increase raids as a quick means of restocking. Furthermore, Sudanese mercenaries who formed part of the British colonial force had mutinied in Uganda. The British were, therefore, scared of increased Maasai stock raids and an imminent all-Maasai uprising against European rule at a time when there was inadequate military capacity to quell them. These would pose serious security problems as they threatened to block the passage of soldiers and supplies urgently required in Uganda for relief operations. To make matters worse, it was at this critical moment that the railway under construction was crossing Maasailand.

Even though Hall, Ainsworth and Captain Harrison had held negotiations with Olonana in April, Hardinge himself was forced by the "Maasai scare" and the security implications of the entire situation, to pay a visit to Olonana at his homestead. Like his subordinates, he assured Olonana of continued British friendship and support. He also dissuaded Olonana from reconciling with Senteu and joining forces with him against Europeans. Finally, to appease Olonana and his restless *moran*, he allowed the Maasai to "raid tribes outside the British sphere, but warned against attacks within the limits of our already organized territories."[16]

Hardinge's visit to Olonana was proof that the latter's position as *oloibon kitok* of the Maasai was recognized by the highest representative of the British government in the East Africa Protectorate. It certainly enhanced Olonana's position at the expense of Senteu's. Even though the Germans recognized Senteu as leader of the Maasai in their territory, they never established any alliance with him. This was mainly because Senteu, in his uncompromising stance, had organized a joint attack against the Germans with his Arusha Maasai allies. He had even attempted to enlist the support of Olonana and his followers against the Germans. Following German counter-attacks against Senteu and his allies, his capitulation and escape from German East Africa was only a matter of time.

Hardinge's visit was also significant in other ways. It was further proof that the British still considered their position in East African Protectorate weak. They still valued Olonana's friendship. They wanted to appease his relstless *moran* who were still an important military resource. The British lacked the capability to stop cattle raids by the *moran*. Hardinge even wished that Olonana's raids could be directed against Senteu to further divide the Maasai. This was the reason why Handinge tacitly allowed the raids to continue. The British were simply not ready to take on the Maasai by this time. Ainsworth summarized the situation thus:

> After a time, when military forces are more organized and our administration is more extended, we shall be more able to edge in these nomad tribes and by degrees make it impossible for them to wander about without permission...
> A policy of gradually bringing these people under our complete control is better than one of using force at once.[17]

During this period the British heavily relied on the Maasai to establish their rule. At this time, Olonana's position vis a vis that of Senteu was obviously stronger; but in the eyes of the Maasai he was increasingly becoming a weak *oloibon kitok*. It seemed as though two weak leaders, Hardinge and Olonana, wanted to reaffirm their alliance to reassure themselves and their people. Hardinge was far more worried about the situation than Olonana.

Olonana is made chief

Towards the end of 1897 Jackson was instructed to see Olonana at Kajiado to ensure that the feared prospect of a joint Maasai uprising had actually been averted. These fears were, in fact, groundless as the Maasai were already seriously weakened by rinderpest which broke out once again in 1898. The epidemic persisted until mid 1900 and its devastating effects were aggravated by drought, famine and the outbreak of smallpox in 1899. Instead of attacking Europeans, the Maasai turned to each other. As had happened earlier, it was imperative that the demographic and cattle imbalances that the epidemics created, be resolved by the usual means, through raids and counter-raids.

In the middle of 1898 Senteu's Iloita attacked Olonana's allies, the Ilkisongo. Olonana requested Ainsworth to sanction a counter-raid by his people but the latter demurred. In August, Olonana's warriors went ahead and raided the Iloita. Lacking resources to stop the raid, the British justified their inaction by pointing out to the Germans that it was "to the advantage of both administrations that the Maasai nation should weaken itself by internecine feuds."[18] British officials at the Foreign Office in London were never convinced by this argument. The administration in the East Africa Protectorate was urged to end the hostilities as they were spilling over to an area under the control of another European power.

Hardinge was, therefore, forced to establish firmer British control over the Maasai. In December 1898, Olonana was appointed official chief of the Maasai, a position that was intended to tie his hands by making him accountable for his actions and answerable to European administrative officers. Sydney Langford Hinde was appointed Resident to the Maasai Chief and Political Agent for the Maasai Agency. He was advised that his role was "to exercise friendly supervision" over Olonana's use of his authority as *laibon*.[19] Olonana's appointment as chief implied that the Protectorate authorities now officially recognized this position as a functionary in the colonial system. For Olonana, it marked the full achievement of his ambitions to ascend to the highest and most respected position in Maasai community. But as Olonana and his British allies would realize in subsequent years, this role was full of challenges and paradoxes.

Chapter Three

A Functionary in the Colonial System: The Initial Challenges: 1899-1905

Commenting on the role of collaborators in the establishment and maintenance of European imperialism, Ronald Robinson stated that:

> The irony of collaborative systems lay in the fact that although the white invaders could exert leverage on the ruling elites they could not do without their meditation. Even if the bargains were unequal, they had to recognize mutual interests and interdependence if they were to be kept. When mediators were not given enough cards to play, their authority with the people waned, crisis followed, and the expanding powers had to choose between scrapping their interests or intervening to promote them directly... Hence the terms on which collaboration took place, were critical in determining not only the political and economic modes of European expansion, but also its agents' chances of achieving influence, keeping control, promoting changes and containing xenophobic reaction.[1]

Robinson's statement is relevant to the Maasai situation but only to some extent. It is true that although the British wanted Olonana to perform a collaborative role in Maasailand, they did not, in reality, invest in him enough authority. The British also failed to recognize the interests of the Maasai and sacrificed them for the benefit of white settlers. Consequently, Olonana and the British failed to promote positive change or development in Maasailand. By 1906, Olonana's loss of influence among his people which started at an earlier date was clearly evident. Maasai hatred for Europeans and whatever development colonialism represented also mounted.

On the other hand, Robinson's statement implying that imperialism brought about development depending primarily on the terms on which collaboration was based, is not a fact. His argument in this regard is that when the terms of collaboration are favourable (by which he means indigenous leaders accepting imported ideas and the conditions imposed by agents of imperialism), imperialism's local administrators, including chiefs, are capable of reconciling foreign and indigenous interests. This then results in development. As he put it:

> When collaborators succeed in these complex politico-economic equations as did the modernizing samurai of Japan, progress was almost miraculous. When they failed to do so, as Chinese mandarins and Egyptian pashas found, the result sooner or later was catastrophe.[2]

The crucial point, which Robinson seemed to ignore or play down, is the nature of imperialism itself. As has been argued by Peter Rigby[3] and Hans Hedlum[4], imperialism in Maasailand and elsewhere in Kenya was basically ruthless in its domination and exploitation. It was, in Hedlum's words "a profoundly asymmetrical relationship that was to a large degree characterized by structural violence, exploitation and lack of understanding of the basic requirements of a pastoral community."[5] It is only after taking this point into serious consideration that other factors in the equation of colonial development can be properly analyzed and understood. In other words, we must first of all answer the following questions about imperialism before we understand the role of its agents. What did Britain want in the East Africa Protectorate and Maasailand in particular and how did it hope to get it? Was imperialism really bothered with the interests of indigenous people? What role was played by the European colonial agents in furthering the interests of imperialism? How did the Maasai and their leader Olonana view colonialism and the changes it was bringing about? Was Olonana, for instance, allowed to take initiative regarding issues that affected the Maasai?

The primary goal of imperialism in the East Africa Protectorate was to make money for the benefit of industrial capital in Britain. Therefore, as soon as the British government took over control of the country from the Imperial British East Africa Company in 1895, officials in the Foreign Office in Britain and within the Protectorate, wanted to establish colonial law and order through an effective administration. This was a basic prerequisite for the economic exploitation of the country. It eventually became necessary to make the country productive enough to defray the expenses incurred in military expeditions against local communities and in the construction of the railway. Indeed, between 1897 and 1898 alone, expenditure on military expeditions amounted to 30 per cent of total expenditure in the Protectorate. Yet by 1905 the exercise was not over. It was also necessary to make the country economically beneficial to Britain to justify its colonization. Administrative officials, therefore, considered that the most effective way to solve all these problems was through the production of agricultural commodities, the bulk of which would be exported to Britain. It was within the context of this primary objective of imperialism that the local European colonial administrators viewed the Maasai and their leader Olonana and the roles they would assign to them.

The administration's view about Olonana and the Maasai

Sir Charles Eliot, who was the Commissioner of the Protectorate between December 1900 and May 1904, considered the Maasai to be no better than wild animals and, therefore, to be of no use since they practised pastoralism. "I regard the Maasai," he wrote in June 1901, "as the most important and dangerous of the tribes with whom we have to deal in East Africa and I think it will be long necessary to maintain an adequate military force in the districts they inhabit. Their love of raiding, is a danger to the public peace, and the arrangement by which the warriors do not marry, but live in separate villages with the immature girls, is a moral scandal and physically disastrous for the race..."[6] He believed that although Maasai habits were interesting to anthropologists they were socially and politically abominable. He, therefore, advocated a policy of civilizing the Maasai by settling white farmers amidst them to teach them agriculture and other aspects of European life. Agriculture was, of course, primarily meant to serve the economic needs of imperialism.

The colonial administrators' views about Olonana were important because they influenced the role they assigned to him as a colonial chief. Hall, with whom Olonana had had the longest relations and was considered his best friend among European officials, referred to Olonana as "a second Kruger in diplomacy and lying". Johnstone thought Olonana was a "thoroughly mischievous and dangerous person"[7] while Jackson believed that Olonana's rightful place should have been in exile along with Kabaka Mwanga of Buganda and Omukama Kabalega of Bunyoro.[8]

But Colonel J.H. Patterson, the man associated with the construction of the Uganda Railway, had something positive to say about Olonana although he also thought that he was deceitful.

> While I was stationed in the Plains I managed to have an interview with the Chief, Lenana, at one of his "royal residences" a kraal near Nairobi. He was affability itself, presenting me with a spear and a shield as a memento of the occasion; but he had the reputation of being a most wily old potentate, and I found this quite correct, as whenever he was asked an awkward question, he would nudge his Prime Minister and command him to answer for him.[9]

The views of Eliot and other European administrators, about the Maasai and Olonana, though largely faulty, influenced the Protectorate government's policy regarding the administration of Maasailand and the role assigned to Olonana. These views also made them involve themselves in Olonana's relations with Senteu and Maasai warriors. They also shaped colonial policy towards pastoralism, land and European settlement. But Olonana's role in these issues was also influenced by his own interests which were, in turn, determined by his perception and interpretation of the times. He took into account his experiences with the British since the 1890s when he established an alliance with them. He also considered the interests of the Maasai but only if they coincided with his own interests.

In the administration of Maasailand, Eliot's policy was not only influenced by his opinion about the Maasai but also by the practical realities of the situation. With the transfer of the Eastern Province of Uganda to the East Africa Protectorate in 1902, all Maasai, except those in German East Africa, were now under one colonial administration. Besides, British wars of conquest were far from complete. Agikuyu communities such as the Tetu and Mathira had yet to be subdued. So were the Nandi, the Sotik and the Marakwet. Others were the Aembu and the Abagusii. The Protectorate government still required the military assistance of the Maasai warriors. This implied the need to maintain Olonana's friendship. It is not surprising, therefore, that Olonana was now considered "paramount chief of all the Maasai" even though the Maasai had never had an individual with such powers in the past. In reality, even as *oloibon*, Olonana's powers were mainly confined to the Ilkaputei and Ilpurko sections. It must also be recalled, as has been pointed out in Chapter One, that among the Maasai, ultimate military and political authority was in the hands of sectional warriors and their leaders, the *laigwenani*, and elders. Traditionally, the *oloiboni* mainly exercised ritual power.

Olonana continues to provide military assistance

The decision to make him chief and the continued reliance on Maasai warriors as colonial soldiers suited Olonana quite well. There were a number of reasons for this. Firstly, by 1899 war with Senteu was not over. Secondly, the Maasai had not sufficiently recovered from the ravages of the war, disease and famine. Thirdly, Olonana had not fully consolidated his authority over the Ilpurko and Ilkaputei, many of whom were still scattered. Many of these people either continued to live among their agricultural neighbours, doing agricultural work to survive, or sought work as house servants for European railway employees in Nairobi. Many of the latter were young girls who were kept by these first expatriates as concubines. But a bigger number of the Maasai, as in the preceding years, sought employment as auxiliaries in the protectorate's expeditionary forces. The last form of employment, in particular, provided the means of rebuilding livestock.

Olonana often took initiative to provide the required military manpower. Richard Meinertzhagen, who led a number of military expeditions against the Agikuyu and Nandi, has recorded his appreciation of Olonana's help because the latter on one occasion sent him twenty warriors to assist in the raid against the Agikuyu around Thika.[10] He also had a Maasai servant, Kenige, whom he lost to an administrator, H. R. McClure. It is possible, though not authenticated, that Olonana also provided male and female servants to whites in Nairobi. These early forms of employment certainly had an impact on the Maasai.

G. H. Mungeam and Richard Waller have observed that the Maasai gained a considerable share of 26,693 cattle, 64,853 sheep and goats captured jointly by the Maasai and the British in expeditions from 1902 to 1906.[11] It must be noted that figures showing the number of Maasai who died during the British wars of conquest, though not officially declared, must have been substantial. It may, therefore, be argued that Maasai participation in these wars amounted to inestimable exploitation of labour. Nevertheless, Olonana got his share apart from his monthly salary as paramount chief. The Maasai who survived also rebuilt their stock. Considerations of such material rewards which were attributed to his alliance with the British must have influenced Olonana to have no qualms about serving in the colonial administration. In many other instances he was forced to accept decisions that were otherwise quite unpopular among his people. One such decision concerned Senteu.

Senteu loses the war and seeks asylum

After 1889 the fortunes of the Iloita and their leader declined rapidly. Senteu's forces were decimated by famine and fighting at a time when the administration in German East Africa instructed their soldiers to shoot Maasai warriors on sight. A large number of Iloita livestock died of rinderpest. Others were seized by German forces. In 1902 Senteu was forced to cross into the East Africa Protectorate, surrender to Olonana and plead to settle among other Maasai.

The Acting Commissioner, F. J. Jackson, and John Ainsworth did not initially approve of the idea and it was only after some hesitation that Senteu and his people were allowed to settle under very rigid conditions. The Protectorate administration had known about Senteu's intended migration through its intelligence in June 1902.[12] Jackson requested Ainsworth to find out details about it and, if possible, influence Olonana to refuse his brother's overtures[13]. Ainsworth found that Senteu's Iloita who wanted to migrate into the country numbered eight hundred. However, he was dismayed to learn that they were already on their way. Olonana, ole Galishu (an *olainguenani* appointed chief by Jackson as a reward for the leading role he played in the punitive raid against the Nandi) and a number of Maasai elders, intended to request the government to permit their kin to come and settle.[14] Ainsworth apparently also met Senteu or his emissaries who informed him that Senteu preferred death to returning to German East Africa. The situation was obviously delicate and required quick action. As "the man on the spot" Ainsworth was to suggest an immediate solution.

Ainsworth felt that an influx of Senteu's Iloita constituted a security problem as "under existing arrangements, their presence anywhere near our Maasai will have a deleterious effect upon them."[15] Nonetheless, he also considered the fact that it was too late to turn them back. On 2 July, he suggested to Jackson that "if we persist in our refusal to allow them to come in without permission, if they do, and I feel they will, I fail to see how we are going to get rid of them."[16] He also informed Jackson that since Senteu's people intended to settle somewhere to the south of Donyo Lamuyu, precautionary measures should be taken so that they do not spread beyond this place and engage in joint cattle raids with Olonana's Ilpurko.[17] He, therefore, recommended that a military post manned by one hundred people and two officers, be established near Donyo Lamuyu. In this location, the post would separate Olonana's Ilpurko from Senteu's Iloita.[18] Meanwhile, he assured Jackson, that he would still do all he could to get Olonana to force Senteu to leave[19]

Ainsworth's views appealed to Jackson who reiterated them in his communication with Lansdowne, the Secretary at the Foreign Office in London, on 8 July, 1902. He stated that since Senteu and his group could not be forced to quit the Protectorate, he should be permitted to settle wherever the authorities think best so long as he behaved himself. He hastened to assure Lansdowne thus:

> Your Lordship will perceive that Lenana, in whom I consider we may put implicit trust, is willing to guarantee his brother's conduct.
>
> The Maasai are in my opinion a shrewd people, and Sendeyo well understands that the placing of himself and his followers under our protection is his last chance.... He is aware that if the old enemies of his race, the Lumbwa, the Sotik, the Wakamba, the Kikuyu and many other tribes were called out to fight his people, they would be completely exterminated.[20]

It is possible that these same sentiments that were communicated to the Foreign office as an assurance that the Maasai menace would be efficiently resolved, were used as a threat by Jackson, Ainsworth and other administrative officers in the Protectorate to guarantee Senteu's loyalty. It is obviously a negative commentary on how local administrators ran the affairs of the country. Olonana was denied a free hand in accommodating his brother. As had happened during the Morijo war, subsequent colonial administrators would continue to ensure that they never patched their differences. They clearly dreaded Maasai unity as they thought it would pose security problems. They regarded the *moran* with even greater dread.

Maasai moran continue to scare the British

Part of the reason for the British administrators' fear of Maasai *moran* were the writings of nineteenth century European explorers and missionaries like Joseph Ludwig Krapf. In 1860, Krapf described the Maasai as warlike:

> They are dreaded as warriors, laying all waste with fire

and sword, so that the weaker tribes do not venture to resist them in the open field, but leave them in possession of their herds, and seek only to save themselves by the quickest possible flight.[21]

This description must be considered an exaggeration of the nature of the Maasai who, as we have seen in Chapter One, were involved in civil wars among themselves and were, therefore, too weakened to be a major threat to their neighbours. In any case, warfare did not by itself constitute the only form of relationship between the Maasai and their neighbours. Krapf was anxious to cast them in this mould to justify European intervention in Africa. To make his point, he further described the spear-throwing skills of the *moran* as most extraordinary: "hurling (the spear) with the greatest precision at a distance of fifty to seventy paces, they can dash out the brains of an enemy, and it is this weapon above all, which strikes terror into East Africans."[22]

If Krapf portrayed the Maasai as efficient killers Meinertzhagen, who observed them in action in later years, stated that they finished off their victims in a most grisly manner. He recorded in his diary in 1902:

Once their man is down they use their short sword, inserting it on the shoulder near the collar-bone and thrusting it down, parallel to the longer axis of the body, through the heart and down to the bladder. The length of the sword is such that it does not protrude.[23]

It was views such as these that had influenced officials of the Imperial British East Africa Company, like Francis Hall in the early 1890s and, later, Protectorate administrators, to establish an alliance with the Maasai. The purpose, as has been seen, was to use the *moran* to establish colonial rule. The irony of the situation was that once the British felt that their rule was securely established in other areas, they now wanted to weaken the Maasai and, if possible, destroy the institution of the *moran*. While the former intention was partly fulfilled during Olonana's lifetime, the latter policy would prove impossible.

The Protectorate government had initially attempted to integrate the *moran* into its own forces for purposes of exercising control over them by forming a Maasai company in 1901. It was soon realized that the *moran* were not ready to enroll permanently as soldiers. They preferred to serve as auxiliary forces during military expeditions against their communities for brief periods, disband after payment and get back to their homes to rebuild their stock, marry and settle like everyone else in their community. In other words, they wanted to be target workers. The problem the Protectorate authorities had with them as with other *moran*, were the raids they engaged in. It was for this reason that in 1902, Ainsworth informed Olonana that further raids by the *moran*, even against other Maasai communities, would be regarded as "a breach of friendly relations between him and the government."[24] In fact, when permanent Protectorate forces were established during the same year, the government had hoped that the *moran* would enlist in large numbers as an alternative to raiding. This never happened as raiding continued, to the alarm of the government.

The situation was worsened by the fact that in 1903 ten years after circumcision, a large group of *moran* matured into the senior warrior status. These were the people who sought inauguration as members of the Il Twati age-set. Traditionally, the occasion was to be solemnized by the *eunoto* ceremony. Olonana graced the occasion as *laibon kitok*. The general excitement that ensued led to increased cattle raids by the Maasai against their neighbours, a situation which prompted Eliot to write to Lord Lansdowne at the Foreign office on 10 October, 1903:

> A feeling of serious unrest has recently been noticed among the Maasai, culminating in preparations for a great raid on the south-western part of the Protectorate near the German boundary. The cause of this feeling lies not in any discontent or grievance but in the fact that an unusually large circumcision feast was held some time ago, and that honour requires each young warrior to blood his spear as soon as he has recovered from the operation.[25]

The government immediately dispatched its military forces to

Naivasha to check the raid for the time being. The government also reprimanded Olonana and reminded him that cattle raids were no longer tolerable. Discharging his duties as chief, Olonana, with the support of senior elders, cautioned against raids to the chagrin of both the *moran* and the junior elders. Inadvertently, Olonana was supporting government action against an important Maasai practice. In so doing he was not only undermining the position and reproductive role of the *moran* and the Maasai pastoral economy, but also his own relationship with them and the junior elders.

Colonial land policy and the 1904 Maasai "Agreement"

Eliot decided that the Maasai must move from their fertile lands around Nakuru and Naivasha in the Rift Valley to Laikipia to create room for white settlers. This event further soured Olonana's relations with his people. Its most interesting aspects were the manner in which it was conceived, the debate that ensued among the local and metropolitan colonial officials that were concerned with it, and its execution. Considerations of these aspects of the move led a pioneer colonial civil servant and critic of British rule in Kenya, William McGregor Ross, to state in 1923 that "the whole episode was an eviction (of the Maasai) and nothing else."[26] Many years later, in 1974, an anthropologist, John G. Galaty summed it up as "the most massive land grab in the colonial history of Britain" (apart from that in the USA) and "an incident based on deception, hidden interests and intimidation."[27] It must be pointed out that Olonana and the Maasai were only involved in the final stages of the plans for the move. This was done under duress and in metropolitan, colonial and settler, rather than Maasai interests.

From the very beginning, the initiative to settle European farmers in the East Africa Protectorate was taken by Commissioner Eliot and his senior administrative officials Jackson, Ainsworth and Hobley. Eliot, in particular, encouraged the immigration of settlers from Britain and South Africa by promising them favourable terms of land acquisition as incentive. Indeed by 1902, he managed to promulgate the Crown Lands Ordinance which superseded earlier pieces of legislation that imposed a number of limitations on land purchase and leases in the Protectorate. The Ordinance now limited recognition of African rights to land to that of actual occupation. It also increased the lease of agricultural land of up to 2000 acres to 999 years and confined the leases and management of such land to Europeans. The terms of the Ordinance were very much in line with Eliot's ideas and European concept of land ownership, both of which were at variance with those of the Maasai.

Although Eliot believed that the Maasai were more civilized than other communities in the country, he abhorred their pastoral practices which he dismissed as wasteful, for they influenced the Maasai to occupy more land than they really needed. Like other European administrators, he believed that capitalist agriculture, particularly one run by European settlers, was more civilized and productive. This was his reason for encouraging European settlement. Later, there would be disagreements between Eliot and his subordinates over the manner rather than the necessity of European settlement. Whereas Eliot advocated the idea of European settlement among the Maasai as the fastest way of civilizing them, a policy he called "interpenetration", the other administrators believed that the "isolation" policy of creating African reserves away from European settlements was better as it ensured the preservation of Maasai culture. It is important to note that this disagreement soon disappeared when the Foreign Office seemed to support the idea of creating reserves. Eliot later expressed a change of mind, though after his resignation. Lord Delamere, a settler who influenced a number of colonial policies in the country, and who had referred to the intended idea of creating African reserves as the "Zoological gardens policy", also changed his mind and argued that the policy of interpenetration would lead to serious conflict between the Maasai and settlers which would entail massive mobilization of government forces against the latter. Olonana and the Maasai were neither consulted over the policy of European settlement nor the interpenetration and isolation options. It is, however, apparent from the wording of the 1904 treaty that they were presented with the latter option as a *fait accompli* since it had already been given official sanction.

Olonana and the Maasai were definitely not informed that the colonial authorities had already imposed their own concept of land ownership and use through the Crown Lands Ordinance. According to Eliot and other administrators, land ownership was predicated on occupancy, better use and, of course, conquest. The physical proof of such ownership was a legal document, the title-deed. Besides, ownership was by the individual or company such as the East African Syndicate that was legally an embodiment of an individual. According to these Western tenets, the Maasai and other African communities effectively lost claims and rights over all the lands that were assumed to be either completely uninhabited or only temporarily unoccupied. For the colonial officials, expansive areas in the Kenya highlands and the Rift Valley appeared to be just such lands. The government, therefore, did not hesitate to sell or lease them to white settlers like Lord Delamere who got 40,000 acres and on a 99 year lease and Ewart Scott Grogan who had 51,200 hectares on a 50 year lease. Others who had large tracts of land by 1903 included Delamere's brother-in-law, Galbraith Cole, who got land in Laikipia where the Maasai would soon be moved, and the East African Syndicate, which now owned about 1,295 square kilometres of land at Naivasha. In the course of 1903 a very large number of prospective settlers applied for land, mostly in the areas occupied by the Maasai. This led to considerable discussion between Eliot and the other senior administrators about how these applications should be treated. According to Eliot, two issues seem to have been confused in the discussion, namely, "the right of the Maasai to *inhabit* particular districts" and "their right to *monopolize* particular districts and keep everybody else out". In a memorandum he wrote in September that year, Eliot posited the following argument:

The first right is undoubted, but the second appears to me most questionable. As a matter of expediency it may sometimes be best to make reserves, but as a matter of principle, I cannot admit that wandering tribes have a right to keep other superior races out of large tracts merely because they have acquired the habit of straggling over far more land than they can utilize.[28]

Ultimately, Eliot's own views and the Crown Lands Ordinance proved useful in granting land to the applicants, even though the philosophy underlying them was quite alien to the Maasai idea of land ownership and use. Had the colonial authorities deemed it necessary to consult Olonana over the Maasai concept of land ownership, they would have discovered that they were mistaken. Among the pastoral Maasai, land is not a major means of production and is not, therefore, seen as something that can be owned by an individual, the family or the clan. What is owned is livestock since it is the major and more direct means of production. Livestock is the means by which nature is appropriated through pastoral labour. To the Maasai, nature and, therefore, pastoral land by which it manifests itself, is spatially limitless and impossible to own effectively. What is possible to control at any given time is what happens to be good pasture land within a very broadly defined locality. Occupation and control of such pasture land shifts depending on seasons and the extent of its sustainability. When the Europeans came, the Maasai may not have been occupying certain areas but they still potentially constituted good pastoral land and were within specific localities; they were still Maasailand for they would later shift back to them.

It is interesting to note that much as the colonial authorities disparaged pastoralism as primitive and wasteful, European settlers always wanted to possess localities that had already been occupied and made suitable for ranching by the Maasai. Maasai pastoralists were being used and discarded in very much the same way as Maasai *moran*. The point was simply that Maasai pastoralism was incompatible with colonial capitalism and in matters regarding land, European ideas had to take precedence over that of the Maasai. This implied that the Maasai had to be moved and if they did not like it, and the administrators knew that they would not move voluntarily, a way had to be found to make them change their minds. What was crucial was that whatever method the colonial administrators used to move the Maasai, had to be acceptable to the Foreign Office. The main concern of the Foreign Office, was that the actions of its agents in the Protectorate should not result in censureship by the British Parliament since this might give the government negative publicity. The Foreign Office itself was ostensibly committed to the protection of the interests of African peoples in the colonies, a responsibility that was often, and in this particular case, actually sacrificed for the benefit of colonial capitalist interests.

It is in this light that the Maasai Agreement of 10 August, 1904 served an important purpose as far as the Protectorate government and the Foreign Office were concerned. Its most crucial part was the opening section which stated that:

> We, the undersigned, being the Laibon Chiefs (repre-
> sentatives) of the existing clans and sections of the Maasai
> tribes in the East Africa Protectorate, having this 9th day
> of August 1904, met Sir Donald Stewart, His Majesty's
> Commissioner for the East Africa Protectorate and
> discussed fully the question of a land settlement scheme
> for the Maasai, have of our own free will, decided that it
> is for our best interests to remove our people, flocks and
> herds into definite reservations away from any land that
> maybe thrown open to European Settlement.[29]

Nothing could have been more deceptive. As has already been pointed out the Maasai were presented with decisions that had been made by the colonial authorities as the events that preceded the Agreement amply demonstrate.

In May 1904, Eliot resigned as Commissioner following the refusal by the Foreign Office to approve his decision to grant land to two prospective South African settlers, Robert Chamberlain and A. S. Flemmer. The refusal was as the result of advice to Lord Lansdowne by Eliot's subordinate, Jackson, that such grant would not be in the interest of the Maasai. After Eliot's resignation, Jackson himself became Acting Commissioner between 20 May and 1 August, 1904 when Sir Donald Stewart commenced his tenure as Commissioner. Jackson soon sent Charles Hobley (his Acting Deputy Commissioner) and John Ainsworth, Sub-Commissioner of Ukamba Province, to travel around the Rift Valley and locate a place that was suitable for this purpose and also to assess the views of the Maasai about their removal to the place. The duo separately went to a number of places, ostensibly collecting the views of the Maasai, but actually putting pressure on their leaders to accept the idea.

In July, Hobley reported that Laikipia was a suitable place for the relocation of the Maasai. Hobley then approached the Maasai at Naivasha with the proposal and reported that "the chiefs and elders expressed their acquiescence in the scheme, without any promise of a bribe"[30]. It must be pointed out that the Maasai leaders Hobley met were fully aware that the government had posted a military contingent at the station to ensure that they were never involved in raids. This show of military strength must have contributed to their "acquiescence."[31] On his part, Ainsworth visited Olonana at his residence in Ngong and put to him a similar proposal. It is not quite clear whether this was done under direct pressure but previous favours played a part. Conscious that he was indebted to the colonial administration for assistance in the past and for his position as chief, Olonana agreed to "raise no objections." Ainsworth reported mixed reaction by Olonana's followers. While most of them were in favour of the scheme, some wanted to stay to the south of the railway with access to Laikipia. As M. P. K. Sorrenson has stated: "between them, Hobley and Ainsworth had worked out the main lines of the first Maasai treaty, and obtained Maasai 'acquiescence' before Stewart arrived. It only remained for Stewart to put his name to it."[32] It would also be required that Olonana and other Maasai leaders put their names to it even though initiative lay with the colonial administration.

After he commenced his tenure as Commissioner in August 1904, Stewart immediately held formal meetings with the Ilpurko at Naivasha and Ilkaputei at Ngong. The purpose of these meetings was to confirm for himself the claims by Hobley and Ainsworth. It was his satisfaction with the arrangements for the treaty and its careful, though deceitful, wording that led him to "set his hand and seal" on the relevant parts of the Agreement on 10 and 15 August, 1904. All the main colonial administrators like Hobley, Ainsworth, S. S. Bagge (Sub-Commissioner of Kisumu), J. W. T. McClellan (the Sub-Commissioner of Naivasha), W. T. Monson (Acting Secretary to the Administration) and T. T. Gilkinson (Acting Land Officer), also appended their signatures. Others who signed the Agreement were Olonana as "Laibon of all the Maasai", Masikondi as "Laibon at Naivasha", five *moran* (two from Ilmatapato and three from the Ildogolani) and twelve *laigwenani* consisting of eight Ilpurko and one each from Ilmatapato, Ildogolani, Ilkekonyokie, and Iloita. Obviously, the Ilpurko were more represented, mainly because they were the ones who were to be most affected by the move.

The Agreement specifically provided for the following: first, the Ilpurko, Ilkekonyokie, Iloita and Ildamat, were required to move to Laikipia and vacate the areas already earmarked for European settlement in the Rift Valley. The Ilkapuitei, Ilmatapato, Ildogolani and Ilsikirari, were expected to move to a southern reserve. Second, Olonana and "his successors" were allowed to occupy the land lying between the Mbagathi and Kiserian streams from Donyo Lamuyu to the point where both streams meet, with the exception of land already occupied by Oulton, Queen and Petersen". Third, the Agreement provided for a road connecting Laikipia and the southern reserve to enable the Maasai in the two reserves to communicate and to move their stock to and fro. Finally, the Maasai were allowed to retain control of at least thirteen square kilometres of land for purposes of carrying

54

out ceremonies such as *eunoto*. The last two provisions were included in the Agreement to indicate that the colonial authorities were mindful of very important Maasai interests. Nevertheless, the Agreement, had a number of weaknesses.

It should be pointed out that the Maasai never actually "agreed" with the intentions and provisions of the Agreement. Those who were made to sign it were not even representative of all the Maasai. This was the case with even Olonana, the main Maasai signatory, whose designation as paramount chief was fiction rather than a reality. Moreover, the intended confinement of the Maasai to the reserve was antithetical to their pastoralist practices which required localities without boundaries. The setting of reserve boundaries was also intended to confine Olonana and his children who, as descendants of the *inkidongi*, were traditionally free to reside anywhere in Maasailand. These weaknesses of the Agreement were partly responsible for the problems the colonial authorities faced in the implementation of the Maasai move to Laikipia.

One of the problems was the refusal of some of the Maasai, particularly the Iloita and the Ildamat, and a good number of the Ilpurko and the Ilkekonyokie, to move to Laikipia. The first two sections may have refused to move because they were not represented in the Agreement. But, like the others, their refusal was largely due to the fact that grazing grounds in Laikipia were quickly crowded and at this time inferior to the ones to the south of the railway. The other problem was failure of the colonial government itself to set aside land for the road connecting the two reserves and for the Maasai rituals as had been promised in the Agreement. Furthermore, after only three years of the Maasai move to Laikipia, European settlers began to covet the place and demand that the Maasai be removed from the area. The colonial government would once again concede to settler demands despite the pledge that the 1904 Agreement would "be enduring so long as the Maasai as a race shall exist."[33]

By signing the 1904 Agreement and even influencing some of the

55

Maasai to move to Laikipia, Olonana, therefore, inadvertently associated himself with British imperialism's "deception, hidden interests and intimidation." The majority of the Maasai were bound to consider him, with justification, as a sell-out. From Olonana's perspective there was almost no option. He was aware that the military resources of the colonial authorities, which had enabled him to ascend to his present position, were much greater than those of the Maasai. In his judgement, the best thing for himself and his people was to maintain the Anglo-Maasai alliance in the hope of securing even bigger dividends. Like some chiefs in other parts of the country, Olonana became anxious to promote other aspects of European imperialism: Christianity and western education.

Olonana's initiatives in Western education

Christianity and western education were introduced among the Maasai by the African Inland Mission (AIM). This was an interdenominational society established by Peter Scott Cameroon among the Akamba at Nzaui in 1895.[34] Its origins were associated with the religious revivalism that took place in the United States of America during the second half of the nineteenth century led by the evangelist Dwight L. Moody. "A socially conservative, fundamentalist, evangelical, and bible-centred movement."[35] The AIM's primary objective was to convert Africans to Christianity and to teach them what they considered to be civilized living. Scott never lived to see the AIM fulfil its mission. He died in 1896 and was succeeded by C. E. Hurlbert who oversaw AIM activities for the next twenty seven years. In 1903 the AIM opened its station in Kijabe to facilitate evangelization among the Agikuyu and the Maasai. The station was placed under the charge of John W. Stauffacher, a young American evangelist from Illinois. Stauffacher, who was later joined by his wife Florence Minch, would serve among the Maasai for close to thirty years. It was with him that Olonana established relations.

Olonana's decision to welcome the AIM and Maasai response to their activities should be understood within the following context: earlier Maasai contacts with Europeans and Olonana's personal relations with British administrators; the attitudes, aims and activities of the AIM; and, finally, the immediate impact of the forced relocation of the Maasai from their good pastures in the Nakuru-Naivasha area to Laikipia following the 1904 Agreement. It is important to analyze Olonana's and Maasai responses to the advent of the AIM within this wider context to reveal the fallacy of the simplistic view that, as a community, the Maasai are "resistant to change". It will be demonstrated here that it was the western forces of change like Christianity and education that failed to comprehend and accommodate Maasai society and culture. Even before the coming of AIM, the Maasai had made efforts to find out if European explorers, British administrators and other missionaries had something of value for them. Indeed in their rational calculations they invariably considered whether or not social and economic benefits accrued from adopting the foreign ideas and cultures. A few cases illustrate Maasai experiences with the agents of westernism and their influence on their responses to the AIM.[36]

Nakuldo, an Ilkekonyokie Maasai, accompanied the explorer, Count Teleki, on an expedition to Lake Turkana in the 1880s. Later this individual became a convert of the AIM and learnt the English language so fast that missionaries nicknamed him "professor". There is also the case of Shanga who travelled to Uganda in the late 1880s, and encountered the Church Missionary Society (CMS) evangelists. He got converted and received the baptismal name, Josiah. Josiah travelled with the CMS members and witnessed the murder of Bishop Hannington. Back in Masaailand he became one of the first converts of the AIM. The conversion of these two individuals to Christianity must have been prompted by the fact that they were imbued with the spirit of adventure and the desire to acquire new knowledge. The new knowledge was required for purposes of reinterpreting the world.

In one other case the choice to become a Christian was a very difficult one. It involved Molonket Olokorinya ole Sempele, an *olaiguenani* of the Il Tareto age-set. For ole Sempele, the road to the AIM started in 1900 while he was on a business trip to Uganda. He met a group of European missionaries whose alternative interpretation of the world greatly fascinated him. Three years later, he went to Kijabe in the company of two other Maasai and informed Stauffacher that they were eager to convert to Christianity and learn to read and write. Ole Sempele was relinquishing his prestigious position to become an educated Maasai Christian. This earned him the ire of both his age mates and Maasai elders who threatened him with, and actually administered, the full Maasai curse on him as was customarily done to errant members of the community. Undeterred, ole Sempele joined the Stauffachers and established with them relations that lasted several years.

In their own individual ways, Nakuldo, Shanga and ole Sempele were, therefore, motivated by adventurism and the desire for new knowledge. As to whether this new knowledge would be relevant to the local Maasai situation was, of course, another matter. What these cases illustrate is that even at the beginning of the twentieth century the Maasai were not "resistant to change". They were eager to find out what the new influences were all about. Olonana's own cousin, Agale ole Guriso, was among the first AIM converts at Kijabe. He arranged the first meeting between Olonana and Stauffacher.

Olonana first met Stauffacher sometime in 1904. To him Stauffacher was not any different from the British administrators with whom he had established relations that had helped him accede to power and helped his people rebuild their livestock. He must have reasoned that if Stauffacher carried out AIM activities among the Maasai they would gain materially. Little did he suspect at this juncture that AIM interests were incompatible with those of the Maasai. He, therefore, welcomed the AIM to establish a station among his people. Arrangements were made for the second meeting at which the modalities of expanding AIM work among the Maasai would be discussed.

The meeting took place in June 1905 and was attended by Olonana, Stauffacher, John Ainsworth and thirty Maasai elders, including Senteu. Considered by Kenneth King as "one of the earliest summit meetings on African education in Kenya,"[37] the meeting resolved the following: the AIM school was to be established at Ngong; forty young Maasai were to be the pioneers of the school; the cost of maintaining these pupils was to be borne by their parents; the pupils were to be taught the Christian religion and agriculture; and, finally, Stauffacher would also evangelize in the school's neighbourhood to a community of one hundred people. Olonana and the Maasai elders must have been disappointed by the curriculum the AIM intended for them. It had no relevance to their livestock economy. Instead, Stauffacher intended to instruct the Maasai youth in agriculture, an activity for which they had very little regard. He strongly believed that "only as the Maasai begin cultivation and industry… can they hope to exist as a tribe."[38] Rather than build on Maasai economic and cultural heritage, the AIM wanted the Maasai to give it up. The Maasai would not pay such a high price at a time when they had every reason to distrust the white intruders.

The attitude of distrust was brought about by the forced relocation of large numbers of the Maasai from their fertile grazing grounds on the floor of the Rift Valley to Laikipia after August 1904. Attempts by some families to move from Laikipia back to their pastures were dealt with by the colonial state in the most draconian manner. It dispatched its soldiers to the area with instructions to burn the villages and confiscate large numbers of livestock. In the words of the administration, "some pressure had to be put on the Rift Valley section to induce them to vacate the grazing ground near the railway."[39] Such treatment in the hands of agents of capitalist development only served to alienate the Maasai from colonial administrators and Christian missionaries. As a consequence, the AIM school in Ngong never took off. Stauffacher naively thought that he would ameliorate the situation by transferring the school from Ngong to Rumuruti in Laikipia.

By 1905 Olonana had, thus, behaved very much as a functionary of the colonial system. In the words of the historian Benjamin Kipkorir, he had become "nothing more than a servant of a system."[40] He was increasingly losing initiative to colonial administrators. As the local agents of British imperialism, the latter now boldly formulated and implemented policies they considered important for the development of the country without worrying about the manner in which the Maasai and other communities might react. Many of these policies would pose mounting challenges for Olonana and weaken his position considerably in subsequent years.

Masai chief, Lenana with his Eldest son.

Chief Lenana and some of his wives and children

Chief Sendeyo, Lenana's older brother.

Chief Lenana and some of his elders.

Lenana the principal medicineman of the Masai wearing the cap of an official of the E.A. protectorate and having an iron poker.

Chapter Four

Mounting Challenges: From a Broker to a Broken Man: 1906-1911

After the 1904 Maasai Agreement, the number of problems that faced the colonial authorities in Maasailand, and by implication Olonana, increased considerably. The division of the Maasai into two separate reserves created administrative problems apart from weakening Olonana's authority. Related to these problems was the deterioration of Olonana's relations with Senteu. Olonana regarded Senteu with growing suspicion while the colonial authorities considered him a security risk. Further, the rapid recovery of the Maasai pastoral economy and the manner of their incorporation into the colonial economy, produced other pressures which led to increased restlessness among the Maasai *moran*. They were reluctant to market their livestock. They were not enthusiastic about western education. Finally, from 1908 European demands for more and better land, particularly in Laikipia, increased and led to plans to move the Maasai once again from the area. In the minds of colonial administrators, these problems and the strategy for resolving them were linked. Once again, as in the preceding years, Olonana only played a subordinate role in the events that unfolded. In the end, however, his authority declined even further.

Administrative changes and Olonana's loss of power

Two major administrative changes occurred in 1905. In April the East Africa Protectorate was transferred from the Foreign Office to the Colonial Office. Maasailand was also divided into two administrative units: Laikipia and the Southern Maasai Districts with headquarters at Rumuruti and Nairobi, respectively. In 1908 Ngong station which had been closed in 1899 was reopened to serve as the administrative headquarters of the Southern District. The creation of the two districts affected Olonana and the Maasai more directly. It brought colonial administration closer to the Maasai with all the implications of greater obligations that were imposed on them. These included the observance of colonial law and order and the payment of taxes. The colonial authorities expected the Maasai in each of the two areas to consider themselves as two separate communities, liable to be punished for wandering out of their respective districts or reserves without a pass. Olonana was still a paramount chief whose position and responsibilities straddled the two districts. As H. R. McClure, the Assistant District Commissioner of Laikipia put it in 1910: "He (Olonana) is as much as he is of the Southern reserve."[1] This arrangement never worked well for Olonana and the Maasai.

Olonana rapidly lost his authority over the Maasai in Laikipia for the practical reason that he could not engage in the affairs of the district. In fact, his attempts to do so immediately after the creation of the new district, alienated him from MacAllister, a junior administrator. It also created a rift between him and the newly appointed chiefs like Masikondi and Ole Galishu who did not approve of what they considered his interference in the affairs of the district.[2] As a consequence, Olonana stopped visiting the district even though many of his Ilpurko people had taken up residence there in 1904. The creation of the new district further encouraged the emergence of other medicinemen. These included individuals like ole Morombo, ole Naimodo and ole Samnawela. They healed livestock, made rain and prophesied. In addition to these practices, Olonana also cured barren women. But he could only carry out these activities in the Southern Reserve where administrative boundaries and his official duties effectively confined him.

This is not to suggest that all was well for Olonana in the Southern district. As in Laikipia, colonial authorities appointed a number of *moran* and *ilaigwenani* as chiefs, headmen and retainers. These people were charged with the responsibility of collecting taxes and administering justice. This implies that they were officially recognized as alternative centres of power. They carried out their duties free from traditional sanctions and, in most cases, without reference to Olonana.

It was quite clear that the good old days when Olonana's patron-client relations with the *moran* and the *ilaigwenani* served his interests were over. The relationship that mattered for these people was the one with European administrators even though the latter complained about their inefficiency and sometimes preferred to visit Maasai homesteads themselves to collect tax.[3] In their eagerness to maximize tax collections, these administrators even forced uncircumcised boys to pay tax as the warriors were not always easy to find in the homesteads. The colonial administrators also invoked the Collective Punishments Ordinance to sanction the confiscation of large numbers of livestock as fines against cattle raids, and other violations of colonial law.

These practices made the colonial administration, and the people who were associated with it, quite unpopular among the Maasai. Although Olonana was not directly involved in these activities he was perceived as an accomplice by the Maasai who expected him to protect them against the colonial "cattle rustlers", as the administrators were perceived. Olonana's failure to do this further eroded his popularity and authority. What most Maasai never appreciated was the fact that the colonial authorities never consulted Olonana about any major decisions regarding tax collection and the administration of justice. As a matter of fact, he was not even entrusted with any responsibilities at the headquarters in Ngong. In the absence of administrative officers there, the practice was to hand over the station even to the most junior white man. For instance, J. Fernandez, the District Clerk, performed the functions of the District Commissioner between April and July 1910 when E. C. Crewe Read, the DC of the Southern District, was on leave.

The impact of changes in the pastoral economy

Changes in the Maasai pastoral economy also undermined Olonana's position. There was a general increase in the number of livestock in Maasailand soon after 1905 despite their massive loss of good land the previous year and the outbreak of *pleuro-pneumonia* in 1906. By

1907 the stock population in Laikipia alone was estimated by A. J. M. Collyer, the DC at Rumuruti, to be about 70,000 cattle and 117,100 sheep and goats.[4] Stock population in the Southern District was much higher. For the majority of the Maasai, the bad times that had characterized the last quarter of the previous century seemed to be over. So, too, was the necessity of their dependence on Olonana's patronage. Many Maasai now doubted the necessity, if not the relevance of Olonana's ritual and prophetic services due to his continued alliance with the "predatory" colonial government. Some of these people must have openly turned to Senteu and other medicinemen for ritual services.

The increase in the number of livestock led to other pressures among the Maasai that strained their relations with the colonial government and Olonana. In the past, the Maasai normally maintained a balance between the population of their stock and the carrying capacity of their pastures. They did so, for instance, through culling as they slaughtered unwanted livestock during ceremonies, and also through trade and migration to new pastures. With the establishment of the two reserves, free trade and migrations were officially outlawed by quarantine rules and the Outlying District Regulations. While the former rules restricted the Maasai from selling their livestock outside their own districts, the latter regulations barred traders from other communities such as the Akamba and the Agikuyu from Maasailand.

The colonial government justified both regulations by stating that if the other communities or the Maasai themselves were allowed to carry out trade in Maasailand, lawlessness would ensue as they would steal from each other. The Maasai pastoral economy was, therefore, almost completely closed from the rest of the country. The only options open to the Maasai were to dispose off some livestock either through the payment of tax or to sell to European farmers and butchers in Nairobi at prices far below real market value, contrary to what the Maasai were traditionally accustomed to.

If taxation forced the Maasai to part with their livestock, official policy which limited the sale of cattle only to settlers and butchers in

Nairobi did not encourage trade. Traditionally, the Maasai did not dispose off all types of livestock through trade. They mostly exchanged bulls, sheep and goats for cows because of their reproductive value. For this reason and because of unfavourable market conditions, most Maasai simply refused to part with their stock. These realities were not considered by colonial administrators who constantly complained, for instance, that: "the Maasai unlike their kindred 'the Somalis' are not keen traders."[5] "In course of time", suggested one colonial report, "a property tax will probably be instituted and this may possibly act as an incentive to the Maasai to dispose of some of their large surplus of cattle."[6]

A little trade existed in Maasailand during the time, though. During the period 1910-11, over 20,000 sheep were exported from Laikipia, and imports into the district included about eight hundred donkeys and four hundred and fifty-three cattle.[7] Other exports included hides and skins. This trade was mostly in the hands of the Somali. One of the very few Maasai that took part in it, perhaps due to his close proximity to Nairobi was Olonana. He had established commercial relations with a Gikuyu trader, Njau wa Kinyanjui, who supplied him with his stock. Olonana's participation in trade may be explained by the fact that he had also developed a taste for imported goods such as the great coat which he often wore during his official visits to Ngong and Nairobi.

At the time, there were only five small trading stores in the two Maasai districts. Two were located in Ngong and were owned by a Hindu shopkeeper, Bugwanji Dharam, and a Somali trader, Hassan Worama. The others were at a point along the Narosura river owned by J. B. Van de Weyer, at Southern Uaso Nyiro run by Aggett-Bowker Trading Company, and at Southern Uaso Narok managed by the Hindu shopkeeper at Narok.[8] These shops sold imported goods like blankets, Amerikani shirts and shorts, wire, sugar and tobacco. Evidently, very few Maasai had cultivated a taste for the imports.

The pastoral economy suffered as Maasailand was only partially integrated into the colonial economy and its traditional communal links with neighbouring areas severed by quarantine and other restrictions. The increase in the number of livestock could not be balanced against available resources, particularly in Laikipia reserve. Soon, the Maasai required more grazing land. The colonial state hardly responded adequately to the demand. This led to internal pressure within the community and to conflict between the Maasai warriors and the colonial administration. A number of warriors were arrested for crossing the boundaries of the reserve with their livestock. Meanwhile, Olonana's relations with Senteu broke down once more.

Olonana's relations with Senteu are strained again

Two individuals fomented the intrigue that soured relations between Olonana and Senteu. One was Sapuri, Olonana's spokesman or prime minister, as colonial administrators preferred to call him. He was formerly an *olaigwenani* of an IlKekonyoike clan who had fallen off with the elders of this community. Sapuri had sought and won Olonana's patronage and, apart from his privileged position in Olonana's homestead, he also obtained livestock and a wife.[9] The other person was Agali ole Gores, Olonana's relative who bore grudges against Senteu. These two individuals convinced Olonana that Senteu was still envious of his position and was applying his magical powers to kill him.

Olonana, who was a very worried man at the time, as his authority was fast declining, believed these court jesters. He reported to the colonial authorities that Senteu was bewitching him. Colonial administrators who always believed that Senteu would negatively influence Olonana, quickly acted on this accusation. "As I had reason to fear the personal safety of Senteu", explained McClure, "I moved him and his people to the Southern Uaso Nyiro."[10] This was not sufficient distance to make Olonana feel secure. At a meeting with Sir Percy Girouard, the Governor, in early 1910, Olonana brought up the issue of Senteu's exile and the Governor stated that Senteu would be moved further away, towards the Samburu country.[11] Although Senteu later moved to the South of Narosura, Olonana still insisted that the former should be banished altogether from the area occupied by the Maasai in the Protectorate. He was finally exiled to the Iloita country, close to the border with German East Africa. But this action never ameliorated Olonana's problems. Instead, it strained relationships between the families of Olonana and Senteu for a very long time. Olonana's initiatives in expanding AIM activities also continued to suffer a set back.

Decline in enthusiasm in missionary activities

Following the failure of the AIM school at Ngong to take off, the Stauffachers transferred the institution to Rumuruti in early 1906. The evangelists were quite optimistic that they would succeed with their enterprise among the Maasai who had been moved to Laikipia. Their optimism was partly due to the fact that they now relied on the ardent Maasai converts, Molonket ole Sempele and Taki ole Kindi, to evangelize and provide educational instruction. Once again, neither Olonana nor the majority of the Maasai showed serious interest in missionary activities.

The decline in enthusiasm among the Maasai regarding AIM activities was illustrated by the very small number of pupils who attended the school at Rumuruti. In 1906 there were only five pupils in Mrs. Stauffacher's class. Two years later in 1908, the number had increased to eleven: "two small girls, one grown-up girl, two young sons of Masikondi, and six grown-up boys."[12] It is interesting to note the fact that Olonana never sent his children to school even though he had welcomed the AIM to establish the first school at Ngong. Olonana's behaviour was not altogether peculiar. Most colonial chiefs in other parts of Kenya never enrolled their own children in school even though colonial education was primarily intended for them. When pressure was put on the chiefs to take their own sons to school many of them simply forced their subjects to do so. When Masikondi's two sons attended school in Rumuruti, it was certainly strange as it was this senior Maasai elder who presided in the curse that was administered on ole Sempele. Such were the paradoxes that characterized responses to missionary activities in Kenya.

In 1910 the DC of Laikipia reported that : "It is feared that the AIM has not made much headway among the Maasai... The Maasai are not a people who are profitable for missions...."[13] It has already been argued in Chapter Three that the two main reasons for the failure of AIM to attract the Maasai to their educational institution were its irrelevance and the authoritarian manner in which the Maasai were moved to Laikipia. "The mission is paying too much attention to evangelical work .... They would do much better if they paid attention to industrial work and education."[14] The DC did not consider the fact that it was essential for the AIM to introduce a curriculum that was particularly relevant to Maasai pastoralism rather than just any industrial or practical work. In fact, the AIM system of making the few pupils at Rumuruti work at the school farm was vehemently opposed by the parents of the pupils. It certainly discouraged potential pupils from joining the school. The forced Maasai move to Laikipia created much bitterness, suspicion and aloofness among the Maasai regarding the colonialists and the missionaries. These feelings were strengthened when the Maasai were again forced to move from Laikipia to the more dry Southern Reserve in 1911.

It is for the foregoing reasons that ole Sempele's case must be considered quite unique. It demonstrates the fact that not every Maasai rejected Christianity and western education. Despite taunts by his age mates and threats to his life, ole Sempele's enthusiasm for Christianity and education never waned but increased tremendously. He travelled widely with Stauffacher, evangelizing to his people to get converted. In 1909 he sold large numbers of his livestock to raise the fare to travel to the United States of America where he attended school for three years at Boydton Academic and Bible College in Virginia. In the words of Kenneth King, he was "the first Kenyan African to go for education in the United States at his own expense."[15] He did this when participation in cattle raids and ceremonies like the *eunoto* was a valued credential for becoming a Maasai. The colonial authorities involved Olonana in their efforts to control or end these activities.

Unrest among the Maasai and the *eunoto* affair

The persistence of these actions, apart from signifying the lack of Maasai interest in western education and Christianity, also indicated the existence of underlying tensions that accompanied changes in the pastoral economy. The serious fight between the junior and senior *moran* in Laikipia in 1906, in which several people lost their lives, may have been a manifestation of the tensions. The event occurred at a time when the Protectorate administration was considering doing away with Maasai auxiliaries and even disbanding the warriors from the regular colonial forces. This decision was influenced by the fact that the wars of colonial conquest were quickly drawing to an end. It was, therefore, no longer necessary to maintain a force to be paid from the Protectorate's revenue now that there would be no more massive official cattle raids by which to reward them.

Why did the colonial authorities target the Maasai in particular for discharge? C. W. Hobley, a former administrator, later commented about Maasai warriors as follows:

> Maasai warriors, when in former days they were employed as allies on expeditions, were often subject to curious seizures. These generally occurred when the men were drawn up for inspection. A man would suddenly begin to twitch all over, he would then seize his shield and dash out of the ranks, stabbing imaginary enemies with his spear. His comrades were quite accustomed to these attacks, and two or three would rush after him dextrously, throw him, disarm him, and then sit on his body. He would lie prone for about ten minutes twitching and foaming slightly in the mouth, and eventually recover, looking somewhat dazed. These attacks, to the lay observer, would appear to be epileptic in character.[16]

It is obvious that the colonial administrators never understood the fact that this behaviour was part of Maasai warrior's preparedness for combat. But their misunderstanding aside, the administrators still feared Maasai warriors and believed that if they remained in the armed forces they would one day mutiny. They also believed that they could not be disciplined. The behaviour described by Hobley simply confirmed the beliefs and fears of the colonial administrators. These provided the justification for the reluctance to recruit the Maasai into the colonial army after 1908.

This general fear of Maasai warriors influenced the manner in which the Protectorate administration handled the disagreement that arose between Olonana and Maasai elders and *moran* over the *eunoto* ceremony in 1909. It is also possible that the disagreement was another reflection of a serious social tension among the Maasai at the time. Richard Waller's argument that the situation arose from conflict over Olonana's attempt to use the occasion to suit his own interests and that the major implication of the debacle was that Olonana's ritual authority had substantially declined, is correct but only tells part of a bigger story.[17] It does not consider the contribution to the incident of factors such as colonial regulations regarding pastoralism and the forced Maasai move to Laikipia.

Sometime in July 1909, S. S. Bagge, the Naivasha Provincial Commissioner, paid a routine visit to Rumuruti station. Among the matters he attended to was the request by the Maasai that their junior *moran* be permitted to trek with their cattle to Kinangop later in the year to hold the *eunoto* ceremony to mark the establishment of the Iltwati age-set. He consented to the request and instructed the DC Laikipia to make the necessary arrangements for the occasion. This entailed alerting European farmers through whose land the *moran* would be passing with their large herds of cattle and the Taylor brothers on whose land the ceremony would be held. This, the DC did in August. Unlike during the previous occasion in 1903 when the ceremony was last held, the colonial administration was very much concerned with, and had to be consulted over, an essentially Maasai affair. And to ascertain that the Maasai never violated an imposed colonial law and order, the DC and twenty police officers stationed themselves at Ol Donyo Lerogi.

The intended gathering of all the *moran* from Laikipia and the Southern District at Ol Donyo Lerogi, before their procession to Kinangop, never occurred. The reason for this was a disagreement between Olonana and Purko elders over the *ilaigwenani* for the occasion. Whereas Olonana chose ole Goinyo, the elders' choice was ole Laikotikosh.[18] Neither accepted the other's choice. The disagreement forced each nominee to lead his *moran* in a different direction: Ole Goinyo's group went south while Ole Laikotikosh's followers remained in Laikipia. This disagreement reflected not only the split that the creation of the two districts had caused among the Ilpurko but also the decline in Olonana's authority and the elders' respect for him.

An attempt was soon made to find a way out of the impasse. A consensus was reached in November that the two groups must congregate, once again, at Ol Donyo Lerogi as earlier planned before proceeding to Kinangop. Again the plan failed despite the fact that Adams, an assistant District Officer at Rumuruti, was ready to oversee all stages of the ceremony. This time the snag was caused by quarantine imposed by the Veterinary Department against cattle movement. It was not until January 1910 that this restriction was lifted and the *moran* allowed to proceed with the ceremony as planned earlier. It was at this crucial juncture that Olonana complained to McClure, the DC Maasai Southern Reserve District, that the *moran* intended to carry out the *eunoto* ceremony at Kinangop without his permission. He also requested McClure to convey to Sir Percy Girouard, the Governor, his wish that all the Purko *moran* in Laikipia should hold their ceremony close to his homestead near Ngong. This was granted but Masikondi and ole Galishu, the two major chiefs in Laikipia, were strongly opposed to Olonana' arrangement.

At the beginning of February, Girouard, therefore, summoned Olonana and the two chiefs to Government House, Nairobi, to settle the matter.[19] The Governor applied the "divide and rule" strategy perfectly well on the occasion. He first called Olonana and explained to him that it had been due to quarantine restrictions that other Maasai had not been allowed to attend the ceremony in Kinangop. Olonana then requested that the ceremony should then be transferred to Ngong, a request that Girouard granted. As will be seen later, he also raised, with Olonana, the issue of moving the Maasai from Laikipia to the Southern District. He then summoned Masikondi and ole Galishu whom he ordered to go to Ngong for the ceremony. He also instructed them to acknowledge Olonana's authority as the Paramount chief through whom he would convey all his orders.

Later in February, immediately after the meeting with Girouard, large numbers of Ilpurko *moran* trekked with their livestock (which numbered about 10,000) to the Southern District for the ceremony which was finally held shortly afterwards. It was obvious that Girouard's permission to have the ceremony held in Ngong was part of his plan to effect the Maasai eviction from Laikipia to the Southern reserve. The *moran* who had attended the ceremonies were never permitted to go back to Laikipia.

"Negotiations" for Maasai movement from Laikipia

Girouard erroneously linked the *eunoto* affair and the need to strengthen Olonana's authority with the second Maasai move. He was simply looking for an excuse to alienate more land for European settlement. About three years before Girouard was posted to the country as governor, his predecessor, Sir James Hayes Sadler, had been faced with a new wave of white settler demands for land. Like Stewart and Jackson, Sadler and Girouard believed firmly in the development of the East African Protectorate as a settler country. They, therefore, had no qualms about increasing the number of white settlers in the country. In respect to Laikipia, the main problem was the section in the 1904

Agreement with the Maasai, which stated that "the settlement now arrived at shall be so long enduring so long as the Maasai as a race shall exist, and that European or other settlers shall not be allowed to take up the land in the (Maasai) settlements."[20] How would white settlers be given land in Laikipia without appearing to ignore their own solemn pledge to the Maasai?

Even if the Maasai signatories had not fully understood the contents of the 1904 Agreement, and they actually did not, there were fears that questions would be raised in the British parliament as to why the colonial state violated an earlier commitment to British subjects. The Colonial Office, therefore, informed Girouard of the need to establish an acceptable reason why white settlers must be given land in Laikipia. What this implied was that Olonana and the other Maasai leader had to initiate the necessity for another move by their people to the southern reserve. This would provide the reason to sign with the Maasai another treaty which, while as binding as the 1904 Agreement, would abrogate the earlier agreement at the same time.

The decline in Olonana's authority, for which the colonial authorities were largely responsible, provided the justification to move the Maasai from Laikipia to Loita. Girouard constantly argued that the division of the Maasai into two reserves weakened Olonana's authority and complicated the administration of their two districts. According to him placing all the Maasai in the southern reserve under one administration would solve both problems. Girouard's reasoning, although factual, was not the primary reason why he wanted the Maasai to be moved from Laikipia.

One only needs to consider the situation in Maasailand before and after the 1911 and the fact that the Maasai were not the only people who were under two district administrations at the time. Their immediate neighbours, the Agikuyu, and even the Luo in Nyanza, lived in more than one district. Moreover, it was not the first nor the last time that the Maasai were in two districts. When Uganda's Eastern Province was transferred to the East Africa Protectorate in 1902, the

Maasai, who were formerly in a different country, were placed under two provinces, namely, Naivasha and Ukamba. It was after this that the western Maasai were moved to Laikipia in 1904 and the two districts, Laikipia and Southern Districts, were created. Why would this situation pose a serious administrative problem only after 1909?

It should also be noted that even after their removal from Laikipia, the Maasai remained in two districts, Narok and Ngong, which were created in 1913. This was done without regard to the administrative problems that had generated so much concern only four years earlier. Moreover, after 1913, the issue of strengthening the position of the Maasai paramount chief was no longer raised. If anything, the colonial government considered its abolition soon after that. The two issues that Girouard was raising were, therefore, real but far from being the main reason for the planned removal of the Maasai from Laikipia.

The crucial reason for Girouard's determination to move the Maasai from Laikipia was the economic one which he deliberately attempted to trivialize, and that was, as he once put it, "to liberate a large tract of country suitable for European settlement."[21] To further this primary objective, Girouard influenced Olonana to link the scheme with the enhancement of the dwindling powers that his fictitious position as paramount chief supposedly conferred. The other chiefs, ole Galishu and Masikondi, were simply forced to submit through threats while Senteu, who could possibly have posed problems, was eventually removed from the scene with the instigation of individuals in Olonana's court and obvious backing of the colonial administration.

By the time Girouard commenced his term as Governor in September 1909, Sadler had already identified the sparsely occupied and dry Loita plains as the place where the Maasai from Laikipia would be relocated. In July and November 1908 Sadler had instructed H. R. McClure to tour the area and report about its suitability for settlement. After the tour, McClure observed: "The actual area available seemed to me to be ample but lack of permanent water was a serious drawback."[22] Despite this serious disadvantage of the area, Sadler was determined that the Maasai must go there. In January 1909, he visited Ngong to discuss with Olonana the issue of moving the Maasai to the area. Reportedly, the latter "expressed himself as being strongly in favour of the scheme."[23] This encouraged Sadler to order investigations into the possibilities of providing water to the area to solve the problem of drought. This was never done throughout the colonial period because of the large costs the scheme entailed.

Girouard arrived in September 1909 when the feasibility study for the irrigation of the projected area of Maasai settlement was still on. He did not wait for the report. In December he visited the Loita plains to survey the area himself. On his way back he called on white settlers south of Uaso Nyiro and informed them that they would be moved to better grounds in Laikipia and be compensated for improvements they had undertaken in their present farms.

It was shortly after this, on 10 January, 1910, that he held separate discussions with Olonana, Ole Galishu and Masikondi over the *eunoto* affair. While the two chiefs from Laikipia waited outside, Girouard informed Olonana that the government intended to restore his (Olonana's) waning authority by moving all the Maasai to the Southern District. Girouard further informed him that the Maasai who agreed to the plan would be compensated with land in Loita, an area that would be added to the southern reserve. He admonished Olonana against divulging the contents of their discussion, particularly the issue of the Maasai move. Convinced that Girouard had found a solution to the problem of his declining authority, Olonana never raised any objections to the Governor's plan. By accepting Girouard's plan to move the Maasai, Olonana was quite oblivious of the fact that the Governor's primary aim was to settle whites in Laikipia. Ole Galishu and Masikondi had been told to obey orders that would be given through Olonana and it was now clear that they were not only about the *eunoto* but also the removal of their people from Laikipia. It was at that meeting that the Governor also informed them about another meeting that he would hold with them in about three weeks.

Olonana, Ole Galishu, Masikondi and other Maasai leaders met Girouard on 24 February, 1910. This time the Governor was accompanied by the DCs of Ngong and Laikipia and the settlers' spokesman, Lord Delamere. In an obvious bid to force the Maasai to accept their move from Laikipia, Girouard told them that those who stayed there faced the risk of being pushed further to the arid area in the north while those who opted to settle in the southern reserve, which would include Loita, would not be disturbed at all. The thinly veiled threat in the governor's tone was unmistakable. Once more, Olonana expressed his support for the move. When he stood to speak, he informed the governor that he had explained the situation to Masikondi and Ole Galishu who had given their consent to the move. Most likely Olonana had misinterpreted Ole Galishu's position regarding the matter since the latter immediately stated that he would only agree with the plan if certain conditions were fulfilled. Ole Galishu's conditions included the enlargement of the land on which the Maasai from Laikipia would be settled and the provision of water. Girouard promised to look into them.

Soon after the February meeting, Girouard proceeded with arrangements for the move. He instructed A. C. Hollis, the Secretary for Native Affairs, and the DC for Laikipia whom he had appointed Special Commissioner for the purpose, to effect the move by June. It was at this point that a letter, suspected to have been written by Norman Leys, a medical officer in the country who was also known for his critical views about government policy towards Africans, caused a lot of stir among the officials at the Colonial Office. The letter pointed out that Girouard intended to sacrifice the interests of the Maasai by conceding to European demands to settle in Laikipia, contrary to the 1904 Agreement. Girouard denied this accusation but officials at the Colonial Office were not convinced. He was instructed to suspend his plans until he signed a treaty with the Maasai.

This instruction forced Girouard to summon Olonana, Ole Galishu, Masikondi and eleven other Maasai leaders to a meeting at the end of

May in an attempt to secure the required treaty. This effort failed as Ole Galishu and a number of other Maasai leaders were still "antagonistic to the move". The governor instructed Collyer to apply a little more pressure on those who held dissenting views. The latter convened a meeting in August where he issued further threats. He told the Maasai that if they broke their boundaries they would be severely punished. He further told them that they should join their kin in the southern reserve.

Shortly after this meeting, Collyer, accompanied by some government officials, took a few Maasai representatives from Laikipia on a tour of their proposed area of settlement. The Maasai representatives were never impressed. After the tour, they reiterated their earlier position that the area was too small and without sufficient water. Collyer's promise that the country across the Mara river towards Kisii would be included on the southern reserve did not change their mind. Their recorded reply was that "if the government ordered them to move they would do so, but that they did not want to move."[24] This clearly meant that they would not voluntarily move out of Laikipia. On receiving the information that the Maasai were still divided over the issue, Harcourt, the new Secretary of State, ordered in February 1911 that the move be suspended until the consent of the entire community was secured. This led to a stalemate which was further complicated by Olonana's death later in March.

The late Sir Arthur H. Hardinge, Commissioner fo the East Africa protectorate, is seen with Lenana, the head of Laibon of the Masai.

Chief Kondonyo Ole Moipei; one of Lenana's successors.

Masai warriors.

Masai warriors.

Lenana; paramount chief of the Masai

Chapter Five

Olonana's Death: Into the Grave ...and Beyond

The circumstances that surrounded Olonana's death and the manner in which the colonial state transacted its business with the metropole shortly after the event, were illustrative of the little regard the local administration had for the personal lives of colonial chiefs. As a consequence, the colonial state which Olonana served quite loyally never attempted to save his life. The medical scheme for colonial administrators never covered African chiefs. E. C. Crewe-Read, the District Commissioner at Ngong, never visited Olonana when the latter was sick. But he quickly went to view his body after he died simply because he had to attend to the issue of succession. For Sir Percy Girouard, the governor, Olonana became important in death, not because of his personal worth, but because of the fact that it was necessary to make capital out of Olonana's supposed death wish. The wish of the dead colonial chief was essential for purposes of justifying to the Colonial Office in London the need to move the Maasai once again from Laikipia.

Death at Ngong and Olonana's wish

By the time Harcourt ruled against the removal of Maasai from Laikipia, Olonana had already been taken ill by what was later reported to be dysentery.[1] While he was bearing the virulent attacks of the disease, he was also worrying over the uncertain prospects of Maasai unity within the Southern Reserve and, of course, the strengthening of his own position. These worries and the disease took a very heavy toll on his health. An administrative officer referred to him at the time as a very old man although he was in his early forties. He failed to respond to herbal and other forms of treatment and finally died at his homestead, 1.6 kilometres North of Kiserian, at about 3 pm on 7 March, 1911.[2] As expected, members of his family and a number of his followers held Senteu responsible for his death.

It is believed that Olonana expressed the following wish before he passed away:

> Tell the Government to look after my children… Tell my people to obey the Government as they have done during my life. Tell the Laikipia Maasai to move their cattle to the Loita plains.[3]

Whether these words were actually uttered by Olonana or attributed to him by others who hoped to profit from them is uncertain. Whatever the case, for the Maasai, as well as the colonial authorities, this wish was interpreted as an injunction. The Maasai respected it, coming as it did from a man they respected despite the fact that his authority, even as a *laibon,* had seriously declined. Governor Girouard made capital out of the wish to influence the decision of the Colonial Office about the Maasai move from Laikipia.

What immediately concerned the Maasai as well as the colonial administrators after Olonana's death was his succession. He died before declaring who, among his sons Seki, Parit and Kimurai, would take over from him. Seki, his eldest son, was only fifteen. He was yet to be circumcised. According to Maasai traditions it was inconceivable for such a minor to become a leader, either a *laibon* or an *olaigwenani.* Colonial authorities thought differently. Olonana's position had to be occupied by his own son even if he was a minor. The next day after Olonana's death, E. C. Crewe Read, the new District Commissioner at Ngong went to view Olonana's body.[4] While there he raised the issue with the elders who were gathered at the place and requested them to name one of Olonana's sons who would succeed him as chief. They told him that since Olonana's partiality towards Seki was common knowledge, there was consensus, that he becomes the Maasai paramount chief.[5] Ole Galishu later stated that he did not agree with this consensus probably expecting to be appointed paramount chief himself.

Since Seki was a minor, there arose the need to appoint somebody as his chief advisor. Maasai elders recommended to Crewe Read that

Olonana's half brother, Marmoroi, be appointed to this position. The District Commissioner did not raise any objection to this recommendation at the time but informed the elders that their choice of Marmoroi would still have to be confirmed by Governor Girouard at a meeting to be attended by representatives from the two Maasai reserves at a later date.

Burial arrangements were made for Olonana's remains. Had he been an ordinary person, he would have been laid to rest in the shade of a thornless tree away from his homestead for a hyena or any predator to devour his remains at night. But because he had been a *laibon* and colonial chief, his body could not be disposed off in this manner. He was buried in a grave which was then covered with stones by those who had gone to pay their last respects. For many years, those who passed by the grave would throw a stone at the grave as a sign of respect.[6]

After Olonana's burial, Maasai elders looked forward to the big meeting while Girouard and C. R. W. Lane, the Provincial Commissioner for Naivasha, decided to co-opt new collaborators to play Olonana's role in the Maasai move. Ole Galishu from Laikipia and Ngaroya from the Southern Reserve, were to be appointed Seki's advisors.[7] The former later narrated to R. W. Hemsted what happened in March during a meeting between himself and Lane:

> When Lenana died, *Maji Moto* (Lane) sent for me to come to Ngong. He called me into his house and said, "If you do not come from Laikipia, you will be sent to Europe and imprisoned there, and your cattle will be taken from you. When you go to the *balozi* (Governor) in Nairobi, tell him that you agree to move. Do not say any more."[8]

Lane later confirmed this meeting. He stated that he discussed with Ole Galishu the following issues: Olonana's succession and his dying wish that the Maasai should move from Laikipia; the Governor's orders limiting the use of grazing grounds south of Uaso Nyiro; and, finally, appointing Ole Galishu as one of Seki's advisors. Although Lane denied ever influencing Ole Galishu regarding the moving of the Maasai in any way, it is clear from both versions of the meeting that he was threatened and bribed into changing his earlier stand against the issue. It is possible that Lane's action was approved by Girouard who was even more anxious about the prevarication of the Colonial Office regarding the approval of the move.

The meeting which Crewe Read had informed the Maasai elders about was finally held at Ngong on 2 April.[9] It was presided over by Lane and was attended by A. C. Hollis, the Secretary of Native Affairs and Crewe Read himself. Collyer, the DC Laikipia, was on leave in England at the time. Girouard's conspicuous absence must have caused some concern among the Maasai representatives who felt that important issues such as the appointment of Seki's advisors and the Maasai move should be addressed by him. Lane's announcement that Ngaroya and ole Galishu would, in addition to being chiefs, serve as Seki's advisors or regents, as they were later officially called, was unexpected and must have upset Marmoroi and surprised the other elders who had assembled. The Maasai had clearly lost the power to appoint their own leaders.

The 1911 Maasai "Agreement" and the loss of Laikipia

What the Maasai also lost soon after this meeting was their land in Laikipia. Girouard moved quite fast after Lane's meeting with the Maasai representatives. On 4 April, he summoned Seki, his two advisors or regents, and ten other Maasai representatives to Nairobi. He told them that they must heed Olonana's wish and move from Laikipia. By then Ole Galishu and Ngaroya who had been compromised, raised no objections. Girouard, therefore, easily made the Maasai delegation sign the "Agreement" of 1911.

The "Agreement" was worded to read as though it was the Maasai who desired the movement from Laikipia. Its opening words stated:

> We, the undersigned...do hereby on our behalf and on
> behalf of our people, whose representatives we are, being

> satisfied that it is to the best interest of their tribe that the
> Maasai should inhabit one area and should not be divided
> into two sections...agree to vacate at such time as the
> Governor may direct the Northern Maasai Reserve which
> we have hitherto inhabited and occupied and to remove
> by such routes as the Governor may notify to us, our
> people, herds and flock to such area on the south side of
> the Uganda Railway as the Governor may locate to us...[10]

Girouard, who had earlier informed Harcourt about Olonana's dying wish, telegraphed the latter to tell him about this new development. Despite some doubts as to the authenticity of Girouard's earlier claims, Harcourt approved the Agreement on 29 May and the movement of the Maasai from Laikipia was promptly commenced in June 1911. It was later discovered that well before Harcourt's approval of the Agreement, Girouard had promised to allocate land to some settlers in Laikipia, a matter that was taken very seriously by the Colonial Office. This was proof that, indeed, settler interests and pressure, rather than Olonana's dying wish, were the real reasons behind Girouard's decision to move the Maasai from Laikipia. Since Harcourt had committed himself to the move by sanctioning it, someone else had to pay for this belated discovery. The Colonial Office was ready to sacrifice its agent overseas. Consequently, like Eliot, Girouard was forced to resign over the Maasai land question.

Olonana's achievements and legacy

What were Olonana's achievements and legacy? Is it true to argue, as Peter Rigby,[11] that he was a sellout? Does he represent the Maasai saying that "it is not possible to hold a walking staff as well as the stomach?"[12] Olonana's position required him to lead his people well by not exhibiting the selfish behaviour of a wolf. Was he holding the staff, the emblem of leadership and at the same time his stomach, a sign of selfishness? Can leaders be completely selfless? To what extent was Olonana's dying wish fulfilled? These are questions that can only be answered by considering what Olonana wanted to achieve, the extent to which this was done and the significance of his achievements and failures.

After Mbatian's death, Olonana wanted to be an Ilpurko *laibon*. This he was able to become, after a long-drawn battle with Senteu. As a result of guile, diplomacy and rational response to the advent of the British, he outwitted Senteu. He was able to secure an alliance with the British who, in turn, gave asylum and military support to his followers. As a consequence, the Ilpurko and his other Maasai allies were able to rebuild their stock and to reassert their dominant position. To this extent Olonana achieved his major ambition. Ilpurko unity came to an end and after the first Maasai move in 1905 when some of them moved to Laikipia. Olonana quickly lost control over a good number of his people. He died trying to reunite the Ilpurko and the rest of the Maasai. The creation of a single Maasai reserve after 1911 set the stage to renewed struggles among the different Maasai sections under completely new conditions. Some Maasai clans lost out. Peter Rigby is, therefore, right when he argues as follows:

> From the Maasai point of view, however, not only was Olonana "selling out" by acquiescing, in a meeting with the British governor Girouard in May 1910, to colonialist demands to abolish the Ilaikipiak section by absorbing them into the southern sections, he was also conforming to the pattern of jealousies and quarrels between him and his brother, Senteu, in German East Africa, as well as with Legalishu in Laikipia, a situation adversely commented upon as causing war and death to Maasai. Whatever Olonana's motives were at this stage, neither Ilaikipiak themselves nor the rest of the Maasai were in favour of this loss of grazing land and a whole section of Maasai in Laikipia. Maasai still refer correctly to this unfortunate event by a seldom-used phrase, *enkidaaroto oo Laikipiak*, which implies the "extermination of Ilaikipiak section."[13]

Although it can be argued that by allying with the British, Olonana possessed better foresight than Senteu, he did not fully understand the terms and wider consequences of the alliance. While his ambitions were confined around the Ilpurko sub-nationality, sometimes at the expense of other Maasai sections, British imperialism encompassed the whole of Uganda and the East Africa Protectorate. Olonana used the British to ascend to a position of authority in their two colonies. In the end, Olonana, though a paramount chief, was nothing more than a servant of the colonial system.

As a servant of the colonial system, Olonana was used to secure two agreements which culminated in large losses of land for the Maasai, with serious consequences for their pastoral economy. This alienated him from his people. His traditional authority among them and his administrative powers with the colonial system, were ultimately eroded by the irreconcilable nature of the two systems between whose logic he was sandwiched: Maasai pastoralism and colonial capitalism. The colonial state used its vast political and economic resources to incorporate Maasailand as a periphery within the East Africa Protectorate which was in itself a colonial satelite of the British empire. This is what changed Olonana's position with time. By the time he died, he had been transformed from a broker to a broken man. To a large extent it can be argued that Olonana simultaneously held the staff of leadership and his stomach. In the end he gained materially as he was officially granted a monthly salary and land as paramount chief, but was considered a failure by the majority of the Maasai for being unable to defend their land from appropriation by white settlers.

Olonana's more lasting legacy is that he symbolizes the failure of attempts by the Maasai and the colonial and post-colonial states to establish a mutually acceptable and workable social discourse on development. Since his days at the beginning of the twentieth century, the Maasai have largely been reluctant to accept the Eurocentric and undirectional type of development that the colonial and post-colonial states in Kenya have attempted to impose on them. The two regimes insistently required that the Maasai do away with the institution of *moran* since it is inimical to law and order. They also asserted that the Maasai should accept western education and the Christian religion because of their inherent superiority to traditional variants. Finally they wanted the Maasai to abandon pastoralism and instead practise agriculture and modern trade as the best ways to acquire wealth.

The Maasai, on the other hand, continue to cherish the institution of the *moran* together with the rituals that mark the individual's passage from one age-grade to the other and graduation to the age-set. Olonana himself presided over the *eunoto* ceremonies that marked the installation of members of the *Iltwati* age-set. After him other age-sets such as the *Iltareto*, the *Ilterito*, the *Ilnyankusi* and the *Iltobola*, were established probably with less pomp than previous ones. This signified cultural continuity among the Maasai. The Maasai have neither readily and wholly accepted the Christian religion and western education nor changed from pastoralism to modern agriculture and trade.

The question as to why the Maasai shunned westernism during and after Olonana's time remains a pertinent one today. Some scholars attribute Maasai detachment from western influences to the power and resilience of the pastoral ideology and praxis. These practices, they argue, are so deeply entrenched within the Maasai social formation that capitalism simply failed to penetrate and destroy them. Others argue that capitalism's approach through the creation of reserves and attempting to impose development from above, has largely been responsible for Maasai aloofness and persistent pastoralism among them. The first view blames the Maasai for being "resistant to change." The second one holds capitalism responsible for adopting a flawed strategy. Neither view is valid by itself.

From the preceding facts, there is evidence of capitalist penetration into Maasailand, however minimal. This occurred through taxation, trade and the activities of the African Inland Church. There is evidence of members of the Maasai community, including Olonana, being engaged in trade. Other Maasai sought employment in Nairobi. There is also evidence of warrior activities that tended to maintain traditional behavioural patterns. There, therefore, existed two opposing forces in

Maasailand: change and maintenance of tradition. Olonana contributed to both tendencies. His supervision of *eunoto* and support for an isolated or reserved Maasai nationality symbolized his traditionalism.

Since Olonana attempted to initiate some colonial development projects such as education and trade, he can be considered a modernizer alongside pioneer Maasai elites like Molonket ole Sampele who defied the anger and threats of his people and joined Stauffacher's school. Following in his footsteps a little later, was Reverend John T. Mpaayei, the Maasai Christian missionary educationist. The only difference between Olonana and these individuals was that the latter possessed greater enthusiasm for westernism than he did.

For many years after Olonana's death, the Maasai and colonial authorities continued to contest his legacy as a defender of Maasai traditions and supporter of colonial development policy. For instance, between 1912 and 1913 Ole Galishu and other Maasai leaders hired the services of A. Morrison, a Mombasa barrister, to challenge the legality of moving from Laikipia. Although the Maasai lost the suit on a dubious legal technicality by which the High Court in the country claimed incompetence to make a decision on the case, they had made their point. They did not approve of the fact the land policy of the colonial state sacrificed their economic interests.

Towards the end of World War I in 1918, Maasai warriors attacked the British administration camp at Olulunga near Narok over the forcible recruitment of their children to school and other policies that directly affected the *moran*. R. W. Hemsted, the District Commissioner of the area, was determined to carry through his policy of modernizing the Maasai through western education, agriculture, livestock trade and the destruction of the *moran* system. The contest over tradition and modernity had been taken to the battleground and the moran who led the attack on the British were given ritual support and protection by Kimurai, son of Olonana and an Ilpurko *laibon*. There existed very strained relations between the Maasai and the British throughout the 1920s.

In October 1932, the Kenya Land Commission, which was collecting evidence on African land grievances in Kenya, provided another occasion for the debate about development in Maasailand. The Maasai submitted both oral and written evidence through their chiefs and elders who included Seki ole Olonana, Lengemojik ole Nakorde, Kulale ole Ndiati, Ntaretoi ole Katato, Keraga ole Satiaga and Lasiti ole Keri. Once more, the Maasai criticized the colonial appropriation of most of their good lands before and after 1911. They pointed out not only the impunity with which the colonial state and the settler community ignored the 1904 and 1911 Agreements, but also the devastating effects colonial policy had on their pastoral economy. After considering the views of the colonial administrators and white farmers who were invited to testify, the members of the Commission denied these accusations. They stated that the Maasai should be grateful that, due to colonization and the Agreements, they were able to survive and become the wealthiest people in Africa even though they made little use of their land. The members of the Commission stated:

> In view of the fact that the Maasai were a decaying and decadent race when the British administration was established and that the protection given them, in all probability saved them from disaster. It seems clear that they have been treated in an unduly generous manner as regards land. A comparison of the sparsity in which their reserve is inhabited with the density obtaining among neighbouring tribes shows how notable a degree of maldistribution exists, and if it is not fair to (ascribe) this state of things entirely to the Agreement, it is true at least that the Agreement is the principle obstacle in the way of ameliorating the position. The whole matter is an excellent illustration of the harm which may be done by locking up a permanent entail of land, and by too great a zeal for security at the expense of fluidity.[14]

The Kenya Land Commission report reiterated the views already expressed earlier by administrators like Eliot, Stewart and Girouard.

The Commission's statement that colonialism was a blessing to the Maasai cannot be justified without qualification even though it was used by the members of the Commission to rationalize the alienation of large tracts of land for use by white settlers.

It is also clear from the Commission's report that by 1933, the 1904 and 1911 Agreements were considered an obstacle to development in Maasailand. The Commission created the wrong impression that the Maasai possessed more land than they needed. The fact is that the Maasai were overcrowded given that most of their land was too dry to sustain their pastoral economy. Seemingly, the colonial government hoped to alienate more land to satisfy white settlers and to further its own game reserve policy. In the 1930s, as in earlier years, Maasai pastoralism was considered by the colonial authorities to be an obstacle to capitalist development. The truth, however, is that by dispossessing the Maasai, the majority of them were denied the opportunity to develop within the capitalist system.

Policy makers in independent Kenya, including the Maasai, are still engaged in debates over issues such as the economic worth of pastoralism versus modern ranching and agriculture. They are also concerned about the nature and consequences of the conflicts between wildlife and the Maasai who inhabit areas close to game reserves and national parks. This is living testimony to the challenges that faced Olonana. Policies that are mutually acceptable and beneficial to the Maasai and the state agents regarding these issues have not been found in many years after Olonana's death. Olonana's legacy, therefore, symbolizes very complex and unresolved issues.

People in Kenya also want to remember Olonana more positively: as a great leader who symbolizes the young nation's educational and business ambitions and dreams. Immediately after independence, a former all-white secondary school located between Nairobi and Ngong had its name changed from Duke of York to Lenana. The school opened its doors to Kenyan African students for the first time. Today a few African-owned business such as a grocery and a hardware store in

Nyeri, a hotel and a veterinary clinic in Nairobi are named after him. A primordial practice has been effectively used to honour and immortalize Olonana.

Notes

Preface

[1] T. A. Kanyagezi "The Medicine man as Leader In Traditional Africa – Mbatiany, 1824-1889: A Biographical Study of a Nineteenth Century Maasai Oloiboni," in *Politics and Leadership in Africa*, Eds. Aloo Ojuka and William Ochieng' (Nairobi: East African Publishing House, 1975) 1-36.

[2] Kenneth J, King, "A Biography of Molonket Olokirinya ole Sempele," in *Kenya Historical Biographies*, Eds. Kenneth King and Ahmed Salim (Nairobi: East African Publishing House, 1971) 1-27.

Chapter 1: Maasailand of Olonana's Youth: 1870-89

[1] Naomi Kipury, *Oral Literature of the Maasai*. (Nairobi: East African Educational Publishers, 1993): 184. This and subsequent sayings are also found in A. Ol'Oloisolo M'asek and J. O. Sidai, *Wisdom of Maasai*. (Nairobi: Transafrica Publishers, 1974).

[2] Kipury, *Oral Literature*, 184.

[3] Ibid.

[4] Ibid.

[5] Richard D. Waller, "Kidongoi's Kin: Prophecy and Power in Maasailand," in *Revealing Prophets: Prophecy in East African History*, Eds. David M. Anderson and Douglas H. Johnson (London: James Currey, 1995) 29.

[6] Richard D. Waller, "Economic and Social Relations in the Central Rift Valley: The Maasai speakers and their Neighbours in the Nineteenth Century," in *Hadith 8: Kenya in the 19th century*, Ed. B. A. Ogot (Kisumu: Bookwise, 1989) 100.

[7] Kipury, *Oral literature*, 182.

[8] Ibid., 183

[9] Ibid.

[10] Peter Rigby, *Cattle, Capitalism and Class*: *Ilparrakuyu Maasai Trans-formations*, (Philadelphia: Temple University Press, 1992) 56. Similar views on social relations of pastoralist production have been expressed by Pierre Bonte, "Ecological and Economic Factors in the Determination of Pastoral Specialization," *Journal of Asian and African Studies* 16, (1981) 24 and "Marxist Theory and Anthropological Analysis: The Study of Nomadic Pastoral Societies: A Review of the Literature" in *The Anthropology of Pre-Capitalist Societies*, Eds. Joel S. Khan and Joseph R. Llobera (London and Basingstoke: Macmillan, 1981), 57-88.

[11] Peter Rigby, *Persistent Pastoralists: Nomadic Pastoralists in Transition* (London: Zed Books, 1985) 81-85.

[12] This definition is by Paul Spencer, "Being Maasai, Being in Time," in *Being Maasai: Ethnicity and Identity in East Africa,* Eds. Thomas Spear and Richard Waller (London: James Currey, 1993) 140. For detailed analysis of Maasai age-grade and age-set systems see Rigby, *Persistent Pastoralists*, 153-157 and *Cattle, Capitalism and Class*, 64 - 69.

[13] Spencer, " Becoming Maasai." In Spear and Waller, *Being Maasai*, 140.

[14] John Galaty, "Maasai Expansion and the New East African Pastoralism," Spear and Waller, *Being Maasai*, 82.

[15] D. A. Low, "The Northern Interior, 1840-84," in *History of East Africa*, Eds. Roland Oliver and Gervase Mathew (London: Oxford University Press, 1963) 303.

[16] John Bernsten, "Maasai Age-sets and Prophetic Leadership, 1850-1910," *Africa*, 49 (1979) 142.

[17] Ibid.

[18] Oral interview, Kashu Sailoji, 23rd February, 1996.

Chapter 2: Olonana' Ascendancy: 1890-1898

[1] S. S. Sankan, *The Maasai* (Nairobi: East African Literature Bureau, 1971) 80-81.

[2] Naomi Kipury, *Oral Literature of the Maasai* (Nairobi: East African Educational Publishers, 1993)165.

[3] Sydney L. Hinde *The Last of the Maasai,*(London, 1901), 24.

[4] Ibid.

[5] Ibid.

[6] Ibid, 24-25.

[7] Richard Waller, "Emutai: Crisis and Response in Maasailand 1883-1902," in *The Ecology of Survival: Case Studies from Northeast African History*, Eds. Douglas H. Johnson and David M. Anderson (London and Boulder: Westview, 1988) 80.

[8] Alan H. Jacob, *The Traditional political organization of the Pastoral Maasai* (PhD Thesis, Oxford University, 1965).

[9] Waller, "Emutai" 82.

[10] The reasons why Olonana established relations with Francis Hall, the British administrator at Fort Smith (Kabete) and the nature of these relations have been analyzed in detail by the following authors: Richard Waller 'The Maasai and the British, 1895-1905: The Origins of an Alliance." *Journal of Africa History*, (xvii, 4 1976): 529-553; G. H. Mungeam, *British Rule in Kenya*, 1895-1912, (Oxford: Oxford University Press, 1966) and A. J. Matson, *Nandi Resistance to the British Rule*, 1890-1906 (Nairobi : East African Publishing House, 1972).

11. As quoted in C. C. Trench, *Men who Ruled Kenya: The Kenyan Administration*, 1892-1963 (London: The Radcliffe Press, 1993) 6.

12. A detailed analysis of this tragic incident and its implications for Anglo-Maasai relations is in Robert Maxon and D. Javersak, "The Kedong Massacre and the Dick Affair: A Problem in the Early Historiography of East Africa," *History in Africa*, 8 (1981) 261-267.

13. As quoted in ibid., 265.

14. As quoted Waller, "Maasai and the British" 543.

15. As quoted in Matson, *Nandi Resistance*, 179.

16. Waller, "Maasai and the British," 544.

17. As quoted in ibid., 548.

18. As quoted in ibid., 546.

19. Ibid., 549.

Chapter 3: A Functionary in the Colonial system: The Initial Challenges: 1899-1905

1. Ronald Robinson, "Non European Foundations of European Imperialism: Sketch for a Theory of Collaboration," in *Studies in the Theory of Imperialism*, Eds. Roger Owen and Bob Sutcliffe (London: Longman, 1972) 121.

2. Ibid.

3. Peter Rigby, *Cattle, Capitalism and class: Ilparakuyu Maasai Transformations*, (Philadelphia: Temple University Press, 1993), 46 and Peter Rigby, *Persistent Pastoralists* (London: Zed Press, 1985), 112-122.

4. Hans Hedlum, "Contradictions in the Peripheralization of a Pastoralist Society: the Maasai, "*Review of African Political Economy*, 15/16 (1979),15-24.

5. Ibid.

6. As quoted in G. H. Mungeam, "Maasai and Kikuyu Response to the Establishment of British Administration in the East African Protectorate, "*Journal of Africa History, II* (1970), 128.

7. As quoted in M. F. Hill, *Permanent Way: The Story of the Kenya and Uganda Railway* (Nairobi: East African Literature Bureau, 1976), 250.

8. These views are as quoted in Richards Waller, "The Maasai and the British, 1895-1905: The Origins of an Alliance," *Journal of African History*, 17 (1976), 547.

9. J. H. Patterson (Col.), *The Man-eaters of Tsavo and other East African Adventures* (Nairobi: Macmillan Publishers, 1979), 228-229.

10. Richard Meinertzhagen, *Kenya Diary*, 1902-1906 (London: Eland Books, 1957) 30.

11. Mungeam, "Maasai and Kikuyu responses," 132 and Waller, "Maasai and the British," 553.

12. Ainsworth to Jackson 23ʳᵈ June, 1902 FO/2/573.

13. As contained in Jackson to Landsdowne, 8ᵗʰ July 1993 FO/2/573.

14. Ibid.

15. Ainsworth to Jackson, 2ⁿᵈ July, 1902/2/573.

16. Ibid.

17. Ibid.

18. Ibid.

19. Ibid.

20. Jackson to Landsdowne, 8ᵗʰ July, 1902 FO/2/573.

21. As quoted in Helge Kjekshus, *Ecology Control and Economic Development in East African History* (London: Heinemann, 1977) 10-11.

22. Ibid., 11.

23. Meinertzhagen, *Kenya Diary*, 74.

24. As quoted in Waller, "Maasai and the British," 546.

25. As quoted in M.F. Hill, *Permanent Way: The Story of Kenya and Uganda Railway.*(Nairobi: East African Literature Bureau, 1976) 272.

26. William McCGregor Ross, *Kenya From within: A short political History* (London: Frank Cass, 1968).   .

27. John G. Galaty, "Interest and Ideology in Colonial Decision-Making: The Case of the Maasai Moves," Paper presented at the Bureau of Educational Research, University of Nairobi (1974)5.

28. As quoted in Elspeth Huxley, *White Man's Country: Lord Delamere and the Making of Kenya* (Nairobi: Chatto and Windus, 1980) 126-127.

29. Colony and Protectorate of Kenya, *Report of the Kenya Land Commission* (Nairobi: Government Printer, 1933) 572.

30. As quoted in M. P. K. Sorrenson, *Origins of European settlement in Kenya* (Nairobi: Oxford University Press, 1968) 194.

31. Ibid., 194.

32. Ibid.

33. Colony and Protectorate of Kenya, *Report of the Kenya Land Commission*, 573.

34. David B. Batret, George K. Mambo, Janice McLaughlin and Malcolm J. Mcveigh (Eds), *Kenya Churches Handbook: The Development of Kenyan Christianity, 1495-1973* (Kisumu: Evangel Publishing House, 1973) 230.

35. This description is by Bethwell A. Ogot, *Historical Dictionary of Kenya* (London: The scarecrow Press, 181)11.

36. These cases are cited from the following works by Kenneth J. King: "The Kenya Maasai and the Protest Phenomenon, 1900-1960," *Journal of African history,* 12 (1971) 1-27.

37. King, "The Maasai and the Protest," 121.

38. As quoted in Robert K. L. Tignor, *The Colonial Transformations of Kenya: The Kamba, Kikuyu and Maasai from* 1900-1939 (Princeton: Princeton University Press, 1976) 138.

39. As quoted in King. "A biography" 7.

40. B. E. Kipkorir, "The Functionary in Kenya's Colonial System," in *Biographical Essays on Imperialism and Collaboration in Colonial Kenya.* Ed. B. E. Kipkorir (Nairobi: Kenya Literature Bureau) 3.

Chapter 4: Mounting Challenges: From a Broker to a Broken Man (1906-1911)

1. Laikipia District Annual Report (LDAR) 1906-1911, Kenya National Archives (KNA): DC/LKA/1/1.

2. Ibid.

3. Ibid. And Southern Maasai Reserve District Records (SMRDR), (KNA), DC/KAJ/1/1/1.

4. LDAR, 1906-1911, (KNA), DC/LKA/1/1.

5. SMRDR, 1908-1911, (KNA), DC/KAJ/1/1/1.

6. Ibid.

7. LDAR, 1906-1911, (KNA), DC/LKA/1/1.

8. SMRDR, 1908-1911 (KNA), DC/KAJ/1/1/1.

9. Ibid.

10. Ibid. It is worth noting that S.C Crewe Read, an Assistant District Commissioner of the Southern Reserve District at the time, regarded Senteu in a favourable light. He stated his feelings about Senteu as follows: "I hope that the suspicion in which he is at present held will be overcome in the near future when his influence with his people is undoubtedly considerable will be found useful in the future administration of the Maasai," Senteu was, however, never appointed a colonial chief.

11. Ibid.

12. LDAR, 1910/11, (KNA), DC/LKA/1/1.

13. Ibid.

14. Ibid.

15. Kenneth J. King "A Biography of Molonket Olokirinya ole Sempele," in *Kenya Historical Biographies*, Eds. Kenneth King and Ahmed Salim (Nairobi: Kenya Literature Bureau, 1971) 12.

16. C. W. Hobley, *Kenya: From Chartered Company to Crown Colony* (London: H. F. & G. Witherby, 1970)188.

17. Richard Waller, "Kidongi's Kin: Prophecy and Power in Maasailand." In *Revealing Prophets*, Eds. David M. Anderson and Douglas H. Johnson (London: James Currey, 1995) 49.

18. LDER, 1906-1911,(KNA) DC/LKA/1/1.

19. The narrative here is based on M. P. K Sorrenson, *Origins of European Settlement in Kenya* (Nairobi: Oxford University Press, 1968) 197-199.

20. Colony and Protectorate of Kenya, *Report of the Kenya Land Commission* (Nairobi: Government Printer, 1933) 573.

21. As quoted in Sorrenson, *Origins of European Settlement in Kenya*, 197.

22. H. R. McClure, "Removal of Northern Maasai from Laikipia to the Southern Reserve, SMRDR, 1908-1911,(KNA), DC/KAJ/1/1/1.

23. Ibid.

24. As quoted in Sorrenson, *Origins of European Settlement*, 202.

Chapter 5: Olonana's Death: Into the Grave... and Beyond.

1. E.C Crewe Read, Lenana's Death and Appointment of Successor, in Southern Maasai Reserve District Record (SMRDR) 1908-1911, (KNA), DC/KAJ/1/1/1.

2. Ibid.

3. As quoted in Elspeth Huxley, *White Man's Country: Lord Delamere and the Making of Kenya* (London: Chatto and Windus, 1980) 267.

4. SMRDR, 1908-1911, (KNA), DC/KAJ/1/1/1.

5. Ibid.

6. Ibid.

7. Ibid.

8. As quoted in M. P. K. Sorrenson, *Origins of European Settlement in Kenya* (Nairobi, 1968) 203.

9. This meeting was reported by E. C. Crewe Read, Assistant District Commissioner in charge of the Southern Reserve on 11th October, 1911, SMRDR, 1908-1911. (KNA), DC/KAJ/1/1/1.

10. Colony and Protectorate of Kenya, *Report of the Kenya Land Commission* (Nairobi, 1933), 575.

95

11. Peter Rigby, *Cattle, Capitalism and Class*, (Philadelphia: Temple University Press, 1992), 123.

12. The Maasai say *"Meibungayu esiare o embulati,"* which according to Naomi Kipury translates as follows: "It is not possible to hold a walking staff as well as the stomach." She proceeds to explain that, 'While a walking staff signifies the tending of stock, the stomach signifies greedy and wolfish behaviour. "They are not compatible, and mixing them" suggests that one is bound to fail. See Naomi Kipury, *Oral literature of the Maasai* (Nairobi: East African Educational Publishers, 1993) 180.

13. Rigby, Peter. *Cattle, Capitalism and Class,* 123-124.

14. Colony and Protectorate of Kenya, *Report of the Kenya Land Commission* (Nairobi: Government Printer, 1933) 191.

Bibliography

Primary Sources

Great Britain: Public Records Office, Foreign Office Correspondence, FO/2/573.

Colony and National Protectorate of Kenya: *Kenya Land Commission: Evidence, Volume II.* (Nairobi: Government Printer, 1933).

Report of the Kenya Land Commission. (Nairobi: Government Printer, 1933).

Kenya National Archives, Nairobi

Laikipia District Annual Reports 1906-1911, DC/LKA/1/1.

Ngong Political Record Book, DC/KAJ/1/2/2.
Southern Maasai Reserve District Records 1908-1911, DC/KAJ/1/1/1.

Secondary sources
Unpublished Material:

* Galaty, John G., Interest and Ideology in Colonial Decision-making: The Case of the Maasai Moves (Bureau of Educational Research Paper, University of Nairobi, 1974).

* Jacobs, Allan H. *Political Organization of the Pastoral Maasai* PhD thesis (Oxford University, 1965).

Books

Anderson, David M. and Douglas Johnson (Eds.), *Revealing Prophets: Prophecy in East African History.* (London: James Currey, 1995).

Atieno-Odhiambo, E. S. *The Paradox of Collaboration and Other Essays.* (Nairobi: East African Literature Bureau, 1974).

Ambler, Charles H, *Kenyan Communities in the Age of Imperialism.* (New Haven: Yale University Press, 1988).

Gregory, R. G., Robert Maxon, and Leon Spencer. *A Guide to the Kenya National Archives.* (New York: Syracuse University Press, 1969).

Harlow, Vincent and E. M. Chilver (Eds.), *History of East Africa Volume 2* (Oxford: Clarendon Press, 1965).

Hill, C. *Permanent Way*. (Nairobi: East African Literature Bureau, 1976).

Hobley, C. W. *Kenya From Chartered Company to Crown Colony*. (London: Frank Cass, 1970).

Hinde, S. L. and H. Hinde. *The Last of the Maasai*. (London, 1901).

Huxley, E. *White Man's Country: Lord Delamere and the Making of Kenya*. (Nairobi: Chattos and Windus, 1980).

Johnson, Douglas H. and David Anderson (Eds.). *The Ecology of Survival: Case Studies from Northeast African History* (Boulder: Westview Press, 1988).

Kahn, Joel S. and Josep R. Llobera (Eds.) *The Anthropology of pre-Capitalist Societies*. (London and Basingstoke: The Macmillan Press, 1981).

King, K. and Salim, A. (Eds.) *Kenya Historical Biographies*. (Nairobi: East African Publishing House, 1971).

Kipkorir, B. E. (Ed.) *Biographical Essays on Imperialism and Collaboration in Colonial Kenya*. (Nairobi: Kenya Literature Bureau, 1980).

Kipury, Naomi. *Oral Literature of the Maasai*. (Nairobi: East African Educational Publishers, 1993).

Kituyi, M. *Becoming Kenyans: Socio-Economic Transformation of the Pastoral Maasai*. (Nairobi: Acts Press, 1990).

Massek, A. O. and J. O. Sidai. *Wisdom of Maasai* (Nairobi: Transafrica, 1974)

Matson, A. T. *Nandi Resistance to British Rule, 1800-1906*. (Nairobi: East African Publishing House, 1972).

McGregor-Ross, W. *Kenya From Within: A Short Political History*. (London: Frank Cass, 1968).

Meinertzhagen, R. *Kenya Diary 1902-1906*. (Edinburgh: Oliver and Boyd, 1957)

Mungeam, G. H. *British Rule in Kenya, 1895-1912*.(Oxford: Clarendon Press, 1966).

Ochieng, W. R. *The First Word: Essays on Kenya History*. (Nairobi: East African Literature Bureau, 1975).

Ochieng, W. R. (Ed.). *A Modern History of Kenya, 1895-1980*. (Nairobi: Evans Brothers 1989).

Ogot, B. A. (Ed.). *Hadith 1*. (Nairobi: East African Publishing House, 1968).

Ogot, B A (Ed.) *Hadith 7: Ecology and History in East Africa*. (Nairobi: Kenya Literature Bureau, 1979).

Ogot, B A. (Ed.). *Hadith 8: Kenya in the 9ᵗʰ Century.* (Kisumu: Bookwise, 1985).

Ogot, B. A. *Historical Dictionary of Kenya.* (Metuchen, N. J. and London: The Scarecrow Press 1981).

Oliver, Roland and Gervase Mathew (Ed.) *History of East Africa Volume One.* (Oxford: Clarendon Press, 1963).

Owen, Roger and Bob Sutcliffe (Ed). *Studies in the Theory of Imperialism.* (London: Longman, 1972).

Patterson, Col. J. H. *The Man-eaters of Tsavo and other East African Adventures.* (Nairobi: Macmillan Publishers, 1979).

Rigby, Peter. *Persistent Pastoralists: Nomadic Societies in Transition.* (London: Zed Books, 1985).

Rigby, Peter. *Cattle Capitalism and Class*: *Ilparakuyu Maasai Transformations,* (Philadelphia: Temple University Press, 1992).

Sankan, S. S. *The Maasai.* (Nairobi: East African Literature Bureau, 1971).

Spear, Thomas and Richard D. Waller (Eds.) *Being Maasai: Ethnicity and Identity on East Africa.* (London: James Currey, 1993).

Spencer, Paul. *The Maasai of Matapato*: *A Study of Rituals of Rebellion.* (Manchester: Manchester University Press, 1988).

Sorrenson, M. P. K. *Origins of European Settlement in Kenya.* (Nairobi: Oxford University Press, 1968).

Tignor, R. L. *The Colonial Transformation of Kenya: The Kamba, Kikuyu administration and Maasai from 1900 to 1939.* (Princeton University Press, 1976).

Trench, C. C. *Men Who Ruled Kenya: The Kenya Administration, 1892-1963.* (London: The Radcliffe Press, 1993).

Wolff, R. D. *Britain and Kenya, 1870-1930: The Economics of Colonialism.* (Nairobi: Transafrica Publishers, 1974).

Journals

Berntsen, J. L. "Maasai Age-sets and Prophetic Leadership, 1850-1910," *Africa* 49. ii (1979) 134-146.

Bonte, P. " Ecological and Economic Factors in the Determination of Pastoral Specialization," *Journal of Asian and African Studies*, 16, 1-2 (1981) 33-49.

Galaty, J. G. "Introduction: Nomadic Pastoralists, Social Change and Identity: Processes and Perspectives," *Journal of Asian and African Studies*, 16,1-2 (1981) 4-26.

Galaty, J. G. "Land and Livestock Among Kenyan Maasai: Symbolic Perspectives on Pastoral Exchange, Change and Inequality," *Journal of Asian and African Studies*, 16,1-2 (1981) 68-88.

Hedlund, Hans. "Contradictions in the Peripheralization of a Pastoral Society: The Maasai," *Review of African Political Economy*, 15/16 (1979): 15-34.

King, K. J. "The Kenya Maasai and the Protest Phenomenon, 1900-1960," *Journal of African History*, 12, 1(1917): 117-137.

Knowles, Joan N. and D. P. Collet, "Nature as Myth, Symbol and Action: Notes Towards a Historical Understanding of Development and Conservation in Kenyan Maasailand," *Africa* 59, 4 (1989) 433-460.

Maxon R. M. and D Javersack, "The Kedong Massacre and the Dick Affair: A Problem in Early Colonial Historiography of East Africa," *History in Africa* 8 (1981) 261-267.

Mungeam, G. H. "Maasai and Kikuyu Responses to the Establishment of British Administration in the East African Protectorate," *Journal of Africa History*, 11, i (1970) 127-143.

Schneider, H. K. "The Pastoralist Development Problem," *Journal of Asian and Africa Studies,* 16, 1-2 (1981) 27-32.

Spencer, P. "The Loonkidongi prophets and the Maasai: Protection Racket or Incipient state?" *Africa*, 61(1981):334-342.

Tignor, Robert L. "The Maasai Warriors: Pattern Maintenance and Violence in Colonial Kenya, " *Journal of African History* 13, 2 (1972) 271-290.

Waller, R. D. "The Maasai and the British 1895-1905: The Origins of an alliance," *Journal of African History* 17,4 (1976) 529-55.

Waller, R. D. "Interaction and Identity on the Periphery: The Trans-Mara Maasai," *International Journal of African Historical Studies* 17, 2 (1984): 243-284.